A HISTORY OF WAR

A HISTORY OF WAR

FROM ANCIENT WARFARE TO THE GLOBAL CONFLICTS OF THE 21ST CENTURY

CHRIS MCNAB

PICTURE CREDITS

Alamy: 24, 90, 180
Getty: 160
Metropolitan Museum of Art: 49, 66, 79
Public domain: 189, 209, 217, 220
Shutterstock: 40, 44, 112
Wikimedia Commons: 14, 21, 29, 37, 47, 53, 56, 62, 65, 75, 80, 85, 87, 93, 96, 101, 105, 115, 123, 124, 129, 134, 142, 146, 150, 156, 158, 163, 168, 177, 184, 187, 195, 200, 204, 206, 213, 214, 228, 234

This edition published in 2022 by Arcturus Publishing Limited
26/27 Bickels Yard, 151–153 Bermondsey Street,
London SE1 3HA

AD008796UK

Printed in the UK

MIX
Paper from
responsible sources
FSC
www.fsc.org   FSC® C171272

CONTENTS

CHAPTER 5

CHAPTER 6

CHAPTER 7

INTRODUCTION

In 2016, a group of researchers from Cambridge University's Leverhulme Centre for Human Evolutionary Studies (LCHES) made a dark discovery 30 km (18.6 miles) west of Lake Turkana, Kenya, at a place called Nataruk. They unearthed the partial skeletal remains of 27 individuals, including at least eight women and six children. The skeletons showed clear signs of violent death – blunt force trauma to the skull, face and limbs; bones smashed or broken; evidence of arrow wounds – there were even stone arrow heads lodged in the skull and thorax of two of the men. The bodies were not buried, but left where the victims had been killed, by the side of a lagoon, the sediment from which eventually preserved them. The crucial fact about these remains is that they date up to 10,500 years in history. As such, they have been regarded as possibly the earliest evidence of human conflict.

It is impossible to say how, when or why warfare began. Certainly, as this book will seem to imply, the psychological structures that make human beings capable of killing another person appear deep-seated, and transcend time and culture. But warfare is different from individual aggression. War is organized violence between groups, states or societies, typically fought according to a specific objective or purpose, either offensive or defensive. Why it began is rather more difficult to say. Certainly, locally rising population densities produced competition for scarce resources. Prehistoric societies often lived their existence on the very edge of starvation, thus any attempt by rival groups to encroach on hunting or foraging grounds would easily have led to conflict. The combatants would have readily applied hunting weapons and tools to inter-human fighting, in the attempt to gain advantage through technology, as primitive as it was. Early weapons included wooden spears for both stabbing and throwing, their points fire-hardened for penetration; a variety of wooden or bone clubs; rocks and stones, either hand-gripped, thrown or, from about 6,000 BCE, attached to a haft to apply greater leverage and force. The simplest hand axes – i.e. roughly sharpened rocks held in the hand – date back 1.7 million years. The bow and arrow, however, is more recent – around 60,000 years old. The impact of this invention on both hunting and early warfare cannot be underestimated. It meant that killing could be conducted with precision and at range; a bow-armed warrior could therefore take on assailants who were much stronger physically than he, yet still win the fight through skill rather than brute muscle power. Indeed, an underlying influence behind the evolution of warfare is surely weapon design itself. Looking throughout history, we can make a convincing argument that the development of ever-more sophisticated weaponry and armies almost demands the pursuit of war to justify them; de-escalation has never been a strong point of humanity.

What anthropological and archaeological research has established beyond doubt is that by the beginnings of recorded history, around the 4th millennium BCE, warfare was engrained in human culture. This book provides an overview of that history to the present day, charting the major wars, technological leaps and personalities that have shaped the world by force of arms. The underlying story is tragic, the narrative here unable to delve into the individual human chaos, misery and violence that characterized each and every war. The wars contained within this book were fought for reasons far more elaborate than the subsistence conflicts of prehistoric times. Here, we will witness nations, continents and even the entire planet going to war for an unedifying spectrum of economic, imperial, colonial, social, religious, demographic, dynastic and territorial reasons. On occasion, the personal ambitions or angry whims of one or two individuals could lead to conflicts costing thousands or millions of lives. Within these conflicts, indeed any war, the individuals who fight or the civilians who attempt to survive have stories of their own, each worthy of a book in itself.

Looking across the world today, it is evident that war will remain a part of ongoing human activity. This book, therefore, provides an insight into the practice of warfare up to the present age, but we wait to see what will certainly come in the future.

CHAPTER 1
ANCIENT AND
CLASSICAL WARFARE

Between the Bronze Age and the Iron Age, a period of some three millennia, warfare underwent a revolution in scale and practice. Battles went from small, localised affairs to major clashes of states and cultures, fought by armies that could number in the tens of thousands.

The very earliest instances of human combat, as our introduction explained, are fogged out by time, but the discovery of grave sites and rudimentary weaponry give us some scattered snapshots of highly personal violence. From the 4th millennium BCE, however, an entirely different picture begins to emerge, courtesy of early architectural and written records. We enter the age of organized warfare, prosecuted between states and empires who commanded structured armies. It was a shift from which humanity would never return.

The reasons behind the birth of warfare are socially and historically complex, but we can trace some general roots. The growth of major settled civilizations in the 4th–3rd millennia BCE – especially in the Middle East, North Africa, China and India – generated the wealth, motivation and population base sufficient to form substantial armies. City-states, the predominant socio-economic structure, may have been at the vanguard of human cultural development, but they were also insecure entities, the

 The 'War' panel from the 'Royal Standard of Ur'. With their fixed, solid wheels, the battle wagons at far left and the bottom panel would have had very limited speed and manoeuvrability.

catalyst for regional power politics, dynastic tensions, nervously protected wealth and ever-growing material demands. The resulting aggression or fear led to snowballing militarization, not only evidenced in defensive architectures, but also in the rise of the 'army', a large-scale military force representing state interests and with a high degree of organization. The latter point is crucial. To function properly and coherently, an army requires: a clear command structure; defined units and formations; some measure of standardized weaponry, equipment and uniform; an agreed tactical doctrine (embedded through training); and, ideally, a sense of shared mission and morale. The degree to which these are achieved, as we shall see throughout this book, varies wildly across history and location. But for our first glimpse at an organized army, we journey to Mesopotamia, *c.*3500 BCE.

EARLY ARMIES

The historical region we refer to as Mesopotamia sits along the Tigris and Euphrates rivers, bounded by the Mediterranean Sea to the west and the Persian Gulf to the east, and covering parts of what is today Iraq, Kuwait, Syria and south-eastern Turkey. In the

4th–3rd millennia BCE, it was a region of city-states such as Kish, Lagash, Uruk and Ur, ruled by a mixture of theocratic, monarchical and democratic systems. Although Mesopotamia had a spectrum of cultures, it was dominated for long periods by the Sumerians and Akkadians, both of whom would build regional empires.

In addition to its opulence and sophistication, Mesopotamia was also emphatically warlike, as the assorted rulers fought over dynastic succession, land, water, trade routes, mineral resources, borders and cultural supremacy. An invaluable insight into the composition and tactics of early Sumerian armies comes with the 'Royal Standard of Ur', a wooden box inlaid with mosaic scenes of conflict and peace, dated to c.2500 BCE (it is currently held in the British Museum in London). The 'War' panel of the box shows, across three tiers, a Sumerian military force conducting a border war. In the uppermost tier, we see the supreme commander, the king (likely Ur-Pabilsag, died c.2550 BCE), standing tall in the centre, facing a row of defeated and subjugated enemy soldiers. Behind him is a four-wheeled royal chariot, pulled by mules or onagers, plus his royal bodyguard force, the men gripping spears and small battle axes.

The next tier down shows the Sumerian infantry, locked together in close-packed and overlapping ranks, presenting long spears towards the enemy. Each of these soldiers is uniformly dressed, in metal helmets and with studded cloaks. The latter might suggest a form of armour; thick layers of padded leather, accented with metal strips or studs, was a basic type of armour well into the medieval era, giving some protection against sword cuts or penetrative blows. Note that the aforementioned royal bodyguard, by contrast, are very lightly clothed, representing what we would term 'light infantry' (see overleaf).

On the lowest tier of the panel, Sumerian chariot troops are in action, riding over the bodies of their enemies. The chariots, or more strictly 'battle wagons' (chariot implies a mobility and speed that these vehicles would definitely lack), have high fronts to provide forward protection for the driver, four solid wooden wheels, and are drawn by two animals, controlled by the type of rein and yoke system typical of ancient farm transportation. Each wagon has two occupants: a driver and a spearman/ javelin thrower, the latter standing on a platform at the back of the wagon, steadying himself by placing his left hand on the driver's shoulder.

COMPOSITION

The Standard of Ur is useful as an initial benchmark for our discussion of the composition of ancient armies, and for how they fought. If we were to break down the depicted Sumerian army according to basic tactical roles, the organization might be as follows:

Command – The king acts as ultimate commander of the army, although unit-level battlefield command is devolved through successive commanders, down to those leading minor groups of frontline troops. Degrees of command centralization varied then as now, but as a general rule, frontline troops had little of the independence of manoeuvre pursued by modern armies.

Infantry – Ancient infantry – and indeed, to varying degrees, infantry to this day – can be separated loosely into 'heavy' and 'light' types. Heavy infantry tended to fight in close-packed ranks, forming a wedge of 'shock troops' armed with long spears, and, for close-quarters fighting, axes, maces and swords. They would sometimes be protected by body armour and a helmet, depending on the wealth of the army, and by shields of various shapes and sizes (typically made of wicker or of wood coated in leather or metal). Heavy infantry, due to their weapons, armour and closed ranks, moved relatively slowly and methodically, but formed the powerful offensive core of the army on the battlefield. Light infantry, by contrast, tended to work in 'skirmishing' roles, operating with light clothing and weaponry (swords, daggers, light javelins and throwing spears) and in looser, nimble formations. With darting attacks, they would harry enemy formations prior to the main clashes of heavy infantry, breaking up the opposing ranks, or would move quickly to exploit a tactical opportunity, such as an exposed flank.

Mobile troops – By mobile troops, here we refer to soldiers mounted on battle wagons or, later, chariots proper, but as our analysis advances they will come to be defined by horse-mounted cavalry. Mobile troops were used both as a shock force, riding up to enemy ranks and attacking with spears, javelins and swords, usually before wheeling away in preparation for another attack; or as fast-reaction troops, unleashed to exploit faltering or broken lines. Sometimes, they might be used physically to smash open enemy infantry ranks, but this was not a commonly chosen tactic – horseswill rarely ride without restraint into a wall of blades and spears.

This basic picture of army organization is confirmed by other ancient depictions. For example, in the Stele of the Vultures, a victory monument dated to *c.*2460 BCE celebrating Lagash's victory over Umma, we see again tightly packed ranks of helmeted infantry with shields and spears, six ranks deep, plus javelin-throwing chariot troops. Although light infantry are not depicted in detail in the fragmented stonework, we can see some lighter troops without shields, armed with spears and axes.

To this picture we must add 'missile troops', although these can be a sub-category of both infantry and mobile troops. Missile troops were those soldiers who fought by throwing or otherwise propelling various types of missile towards the enemy. We have already mentioned javelins and throwing spears in this context; these light weapons were generally propelled by arm power alone, although there were assisted-throwing devices, adapted from hunting tools, which enabled the thrower to apply greater leverage to the release and therefore achieve extended range. As a general rule, however, hand-thrown javelins had a range of *c.*15–20 m (16–22 yards), but with mechanical assistance another 10 m (11 yards) could be added.

Offering both greater range and, in trained hands, accuracy, was the bow and arrows. Archers were a critical component of most ancient armies. They delivered long-range attrition on enemies well before massed foot soldiers closed the distance, and they could also strike point targets with impressive accuracy, e.g. enemy commanders. The earliest combat bows were 'self-bows', constructed from a single piece of wood. Although certainly effective, self-bow performance suffered from environmental changes in humidity and temperature. They were also necessarily long to provide the requisite elastic potential energy in the draw, making them unsuited for use within close-packed infantry ranks or on horseback. In the 3rd and 2nd millennia BCE, however, we see the emergence of composite bows – shortened bows constructed from a wooden core fronted with sinew and backed by animal horn. By making the weapon in this laminated fashion, the bow generated a lot of power for its size, meaning that talented archers with the best bows could reach targets out to *c.*175 m (191 yards). These bows could also be handled comfortably from chariots or even on horseback. Some peoples, such as the Scythians and Assyrians, became noted for their exceptional talents with a bow, inculcated from youth.

Copper, Bronze and Iron Weapons

Developments in ancient metallurgy had a crucial impact on evolving warfare, particularly in terms of the lethality, mass production and durability of hand-held weaponry. The earliest types of metal weaponry were made from unalloyed copper. This was discovered in the 7th millennium BCE, likely in Anatolia, and was in extensive use in Mesopotamia and Egypt by the 4th millennium BCE, spreading out to India, China and Europe. The problem with copper is its inherent softness, which makes it liable to bend, break or blunt in combat. The solution was to mix copper with tin to form bronze, which was significantly harder and, crucially, could take and hold a sharper edge, making it ideal for swords and daggers. Bronze first appeared around 2800 BCE among the Sumerians, and again spread internationally during the next millennium. There was a downside to the material, however: bronze could be made into glamorous weapons, but it was expensive, and therefore not ideal for arming a mass infantry force. The crucial breakthrough came with the utilization of iron in c.1500 BCE. Iron is harder to work than copper or tin, and in its basic state is softer than bronze, but it had the signal advantage of being abundant. Its value for weaponry jumped immeasurably in the 11th century BCE, when carbon (via charcoal) was transferred into the iron during the smelting process to form steel, which was a supreme metal for making weaponry: durable, affordable and capable of holding a keen edge or point. With the introduction of iron and steel, other metals tended to be confined to weapons with pure ceremonial purposes.

The ancient missile weapon with the longest range was the sling, which used centrifugal force to generate power to propel a small missile (usually a stone, but later small lead bullets) over ranges of up to and even more than 400 m (437 yards), at velocities of 100 m/sec (328 ft/sec). The most famous ancient slinger is David, of the Biblical tale of David and Goliath. David's ability to strike Goliath in the centre of his forehead is not exaggerated; well-trained slingers could hit individual human targets at close range, sometimes with armour-penetrating capability. (Sling stones have been found embedded in the mud-brick walls of ancient fortresses.)

Infantry (light and heavy), chariots and cavalry, and missiles were the basic ingredients of ancient armies. The trick to achieving victories with these ingredients was for commanders to combine them in the most effective way, optimize the power of the men and the weapons, and to apply them at the right moments in battle to achieve decisive effect.

THE RISE OF WARRIOR STATES

Keeping our attention on Mesopotamia, the Middle East and the Eastern Mediterranean between the 3rd and the 1st millennia BCE, we witness the steady rise of city-states to the level of imperial powers, the accompanying armies swelling in scale and combat capability to fuel the political and geographical expansion. We have already noted the armies of Sumeria, but other powers soon began to jockey for position in martial history. Between c.2340 and 2284 BCE, for example, the ruler Sargon of Akkad forged the first Mesopotamian Empire, roughly coterminous with modern-day Iraq, through military conquest, absorbing the territories of other regional city-states via a standing army of c.5,400 soldiers, which included four-wheeled chariots and archers equipped with composite bows. Other kingdoms grew around Assyria, Babylon and Egypt. The Babylonian ruler Hammurabi (r. c.1792–50 BCE), for example, turned upon his former allies in the 18th century BCE, driving his territorial control westwards into the Syrian Desert and eastwards to the Persian Gulf.

Some of the most revealing insights into ancient warfare, however, come from New Kingdom Egypt (16th–11th century BCE). During this period, Egypt – already the supreme power in North Africa – came into conflict with those powers within and beyond the Arabian Peninsula, as the pharaohs attempted to create a protective buffer zone between it and the rival powers of the Levant. The

 This astounding work of martial beauty, the golden helmet of Meskalamdug (fl. c.2,600 BCE) – an early Sumerian ruler – now resides in the British Museum.

consequent battles explicitly show the application of *tactics*, rather than simply brute force and human mass, to seize the advantage on the battlefield. At the Battle of Megiddo in *c*.1468 BCE, for example, Pharaoh Thutmosis III (r. 1479–25 BCE) outmanoeuvred and outpaced a combined army of the princes of Megiddo and Kadesh in Palestine via a risky diversion through the narrow Aruna Pass. This provided a snappy route through the mountains, but was one that his enemies thought he would avoid, on account of its vulnerability to attack.

The greatest recorded battle of New Kingdom Egypt was, however, that which occurred at Kadesh in *c*.1275 BCE. Fought by Pharaoh Ramesses II (r. 1279–13 BCE) against the Hittite king Muwatalli II in western Syria, it saw Muwatalli's forces ambush the Egyptians with a massed attack of fast-moving two-wheeled, two-man chariots, launching the onslaught from across the Orontes River as the Egyptian invasion column advanced north of Kadesh. At first it appeared that the Hittites would split the Egyptian forces in two and inflict a sequential defeat, but an effective counter-attack in the north, personally led by Ramesses, and the arrival of Egyptian reinforcements from the west and south, carried the day for the Egyptians, although the peace agreement subsequently concluded left Kadesh in Hittite possession.

Egyptian power would remain significant for another century, but during the reign of Ramesses III (r. 1186–55 BCE), the powerbase was eroded by the attacks of the 'Sea Peoples'. The ethnic and political composition of the Sea Peoples is still a matter of historical debate, but they inflicted numerous wearing defeats on the Egyptians, on land and at sea. These early sea battles set the pattern for many throughout ancient history. Oar-powered vessels, fitted with battering rams below the waterlines, would be rowed at speed towards similar enemy vessels, aiming either to ram and sink the opponent or to draw close enough for blistering exchanges of javelin, sling and arrow barrages. Ships would also be hooked together, early marines and sailors boarding the enemy vessels and fighting it out hand to hand on the decks. In many ways, these primitive warships were more platforms for floating infantry warfare than instruments of destruction in themselves.

WARRIOR EMPIRES

During the first half of the 1st millennium BCE, imperial might in Mesopotamia reached new heights. Imperial powers not only acquired armies of awe-inspiring size (albeit frequently exaggerated), which in turn placed additional demands upon command and control, but the states who made up the empires also each had their own tactical, technological and organizational slant on warfare. Some states, for example, had strong traditions of archery, while others brought combat horsemanship. Of particular note during this period was the transition, during the 8th century BCE, from chariots to individual mounted cavalry. Cavalry soldiers were faster, more mobile and more tactically flexible than chariots. They were armed with spears, javelins and also bows; despite their undulating animal platform, cavalry archers such as the Scythians could hit an individual human target from horseback while on the gallop.

From the 9th to the 7th centuries BCE, the greatest of the regional empires was that of the Assyrians, which expanded under warrior leaders such as Shalmaneser III (r. 859–24 BCE), Tiglath-Pileser III (r. 745–27 BCE), Sennacherib (r. 705–681 BCE) and Ashurbanipal (r. 669–31 BCE). The Assyrians had a triumphal time, defeating powers such as the Hurrians, Hittites, Egyptians and Judaeans with an army that was increasingly professionalized. At the beginning of Assyrian history, its army was essentially a seasonal militia, i.e. a citizen military force raised when manpower could be spared from socially critical agricultural duties, such as the harvest. But as time progressed, and especially under Tiglath-Pileser III, a larger

An Assyrian two-man war chariot in action, clearly indicating how the archer on the platform could take accurate shots at point targets (in this case on enemy warrior) while on the move at speed.

standing army was formed to enable Assyria to maintain and expand its empire. It was a mixed force of chariots, cavalry, archers and foot soldiers, coordinated through proper professional generalship and divided into a strict system of unit sizes, in multiples of 10, 100 or 1,000.

On the open battlefield, the Assyrian army was a war-winning entity, capable of fast redirection and concentrated force. But the Assyrians were also experts at that other cornerstone of ancient warfare: sieges. In 701 BCE, Sennacherib's army besieged the Judaean walled city of Lachish, the action usefully detailed in reliefs on Sennacherib's palace. They show sophisticated siege warfare tactics, utilizing many of the principles and technologies that would express siege warfare well into the medieval period. Lachish was first encircled, enforcing a blockade. Archers worked in tandem with shield bearers, the latter offering overhead cover to the former, while the archers maintained suppressive fire against defenders on the top of the battlements. Similarly protected, Assyrian engineers destabilized the foundations with undermining operations. They also constructed a paved ramp, over which a four-wheeled wooden tower, a siege engine, was hauled up to the city walls, smashing them with an integrated ram. While slingers and archers fired on the Judaeans, other infantry scaled the walls with assault ladders. Lachish fell, and in keeping with the Assyrians' reputation for brutality, much of the population of the city was massacred.

The Assyrian Empire remained mighty until the 7th century BCE, when, in the second half of the century, it began to crumble precipitously. The landmark event came in 612 BCE, when an alliance of Babylonian and Medean forces assaulted the Assyrian capital Nineveh, which was taken following a three-month siege. By the end of the century, the much-reduced empire was on its knees, and its territories what successively passed into the hands of other rising empires.

Following the loss of Nineveh, other empires and city-states, including Babylon, Egypt and Israel, wrestled for control over the region's contentious territories. Having a large army was never enough on its own to secure victory; it had to be allied to talented leadership. This is aptly demonstrated by the rise of the Persian Empire under Cyrus the Great (r. 559–30 BCE), the founder of what we know as the Achaemenid dynasty. Cyrus was an aggressive, innovative leader. An early example of his military competence came at Sardis, the capital of Lydia, in 546 BCE, when Cyrus' army was attacked by a numerically superior Lydian alliance. Cyrus formed his troops into a defensive square, keeping the attackers at bay with an outlying barrier of spears and archery fire coming from the centre of the square. This tactic so disrupted the Lydian effort that eventually Cyrus was able to launch a counter-attack, and Sardis was soon captured. In 539 BCE, Cyrus defeated a Babylonian army at Opis, then went on to besiege and take Babylon itself. By this point, Cyrus effectively ruled over northern Mesopotamia, much of Anatolia and western Iran. As we shall see below, subsequent Persian rulers eventually met their match in their attempt to incorporate Greece into the Persian Empire.

A few points about the Persian army are worth noting before moving on. As with many ancient empires, the army began somewhat informally, with seasonal forces assembled from alliances of local tribes. But professionalization quickly accrued and developed. Some of Cyrus' reforms included:

- Forming an elite force of heavy infantry called the 'Immortals', a royal bodyguard and the core of a standing army. The Immortals' name comes from the fact that their strength was always kept at 10,000 men, any losses in battle or through illness were always immediately replaced.

- Cyrus increased the proportion of cavalry in his army, from about 10 per cent at the beginning of his reign to about 20 per cent, acknowledging the decisive role cavalry – both light and heavy types – could play on the battlefield.
- Persian chariots often had scythes fitted to their wheel hubs, which could be devastating in a close pass across the front of enemy infantry ranks.
- Cyrus oversaw significant improvements in military logistics, enabling his army to conduct campaigns over long distances. A designated commissariat was in charge of all matters of provision, encampment, sanitation and equipment supply, while Cyrus obliged each local Persian governor (satrap) to maintain ready supplies of food to support military campaigns.
- A professional body of combat engineers built roads and bridges to facilitate the swift deployment of even large armies.

WARFARE IN ANCIENT GREECE AND THE HELLENISTIC AGE

During the rise of the Persian Empire, Greece consisted of a large collection of relatively small city-states, surviving either independently or forming regional alliances. Regular friction between the city-states meant that Greece had an embedded military psyche, encoded in the two great warrior narratives written by Homer in the 8th or 7th centuries BCE: the *Iliad*, which recounted the epic Trojan War; and the *Odyssey*, chronicling the decade-long journey of Odysseus after the fall of Troy.

Greek armies prior to the reign of Philip II of Macedon (r. 359–36 BCE) were citizen forces, all free adult males being under obligation to provide military service when required. Because of Greece's mountainous terrain, the Greek armies generally had little in the way of cavalry (again, something that would change under Philip), instead relying upon hoplite heavy infantry. The hoplites wore extensive body armour, carried a large wooden shield, and fought primarily with a spear about 2.3–3m (7–10ft) long, with a short sword as a back-up weapon. On the battlefield, the hoplites were arranged in the phalanx, a close-packed formation typically about eight ranks deep, which relied upon discipline, a bristling face of spears and sheer mass to push back its enemies.

By the beginning of the 5th century BCE, the two most powerful Greek city-states were Athens and Sparta. Both fielded excellent armies. Sparta in particular had a unique warrior culture, training all its male citizens from the age of seven to be hardened, skilful in weapon handling and brutally fearless in combat.

The military capabilities of Athens and Sparta, and of many other Greek city-states, were tested to the full in the early 5th century BCE, as Persian expansion under Emperor Darius I the Great (r. 522–486 BCE) led to a swarming Persian invasion of Greece in 490 BCE, its principal target being Athens. At the coastal plain of Marathon, just to the north of Athens, Athenian hoplites pulled off a victory that still resonates in history. Having landed perhaps as many as 25,000 troops in the Bay of Marathon, the Persians were astonished by a sudden hoplite charge of *c.*10,000 Greeks. Famously, the Greek commander Miltiades had deliberately weakened the centre of his phalanx line, so when the Persian counter-attack began to make progress there the Greek line wrapped around them, enveloping the Persian centre. Those Persian soldiers who survived the trap and subsequent pursuit fled back to their boats and departed. Athens was saved.

Ten years later, in August 480 BCE, Darius' ambitious son, Xerxes, deciding it was time to avenge his father's defeat, launched another invasion of Greece, this time on an altogether greater scale – possibly *c.*200,000 troops. In an astonishing sacrificial action, 300 Spartans and about 1,000 Greek allies held back the Persian tide in the narrow coastal pass at Thermopylae, inflicting possibly 20,000

✴ *The Greek phalanx worked by concentrating a mass of humanity and spears across a dense front, and advancing remorselessly. The formation had little mobility, however, and became steadily obsolete in the age of cavalry*

casualties on the Persians before the Greeks were wiped out to a man. The Persians went on to seize Athens, but the Athenian fleet then devastated the Persian invasion fleet, on which the land army relied for its logistics and coastal movement, at the naval battle of Salamis. The final acts of Greek victory came in the battles of Plataea and Mycale in 479 BCE, confirming the superiority of the disciplined Greek phalanx over the variegated mass of the Persian army.

While the early 5th century BCE saw the Greeks repel external threats, much of the rest of the century was taken up fighting among themselves. During the Peloponnesian War of 431–04, fought sporadically between the Delian League (led by Athens) and the Peloponnesian League (led by Sparta), weaknesses emerged in Athenian war-making that led to the ultimate defeat of the Delian League. At the Athenian siege of Syracuse (415–13 BCE), limited Athenian siege tactics and the absence of siege engines led to the Spartans not only breaking the siege, but also destroying the Athenian force as it retreated through the mountains. Athens was subsequently clamped under siege from the land, and in 405 BCE the talented Spartan admiral Lysander smashed the Athenian fleet at Aegospotami off the coast of Thrace, severing Athens' maritime lifetime. The city was forced to surrender the following year.

In the aftermath of the Athenian defeat, new powers rose to prominence in Greece. During the so-called Theban Wars (378–62 BCE), the army of Thebes inflicted major defeats upon both Sparta at Leuctra in 371 BCE and a combined Athenian–Spartan army at Mantinea in 362 BCE. Both victories can be laid at the door of the Theban general Epaminondas, who showed a flexible talent with hoplite formations, massively strengthening one flank while weakening the other, to cause disarray in the enemy formations. Epaminondas was, however, killed in the last stage of the Battle of Mantinea, a loss that would go on to cause the descent of Theban power.

Despite all this, completely overshadowing the limited rise of Thebes was the extraordinary ascent of Macedon, the kingdom in northern Greece, under two of the greatest figures in military history: Philip II and his son, Alexander III (r. 336–23 BCE), known as Alexander the Great.

Philip reworked his army extensively, through innovations in organization, training, tactical formations and weaponry. He deepened the ranks of the phalanx, but also broadened the individual space around the men, enabling them to fight better at close quarters. His hoplites were divided into two types: the *pezetaeri* armed with 4 m (13 ft) *sarissa* spears and the more mobile and faster-moving *hypaspists*, usually positioned on the right flank to act as a 'hinge' for the formation. *Peltast* light infantry acted as skirmishers with their bows, slings and javelins. Well-trained and numerous cavalry was also central to the Macedonian army, including the elite aristocratic 'Companion Cavalry' and talented Thessalian mercenaries. Philip introduced spear- and stone-throwing heavy weapons – catapults and ballistae – which were, in essence, one of the earliest examples of field artillery. Taken together, this well-composed army was truly a battle-winning entity.

At the Battle of Chaeronea in 338 BCE, Philip proved the worth of his army when he, and his son Alexander, who led charge of Macedonian cavalry, demolished a combined Theban–Athenian force, in a victory that gave the Macedonians control over Greece. Philips' eyes now turned eastwards towards the conquest of Persia, although ambition was cut short by his assassination in 336 BCE. Instead, it was Alexander who would not only forge one of the largest empires of the ancient world, but also take his place in the pantheon of history's most elevated military commanders.

After consolidating his hold over Greece, Alexander pushed south and east, racking up victory after victory until his empire stretched from Greece and Egypt in the west across Persia to northern India. All of his victories are worthy of study, lessons in channelled aggression and tactical boldness. At the Battle of Issus in November 333 BCE, for example, Alexander used a combination of a strong central phalanx and flanking cavalry attacks to defeat a Persian force three times the size of his own army. A similar victory was taken in 331 BCE at the Battle of Gaugamela (Arbela) against a Persian army with a four-to-one size advantage; again, the Persians were routed, allowing Alexander to take the Persian capital, Babylon. At the Hydaspes River, northern India, in 326 BCE, he unbalanced the army of the Punjab ruler King Porus by sending part of his army across the river in a night-time amphibious manoeuvre, and used light javelin troops to panic enemy war elephants, before a combined cavalry and infantry charge took the field.

As well as being a talented tactician, Alexander also had the virtue of intelligence in strategy. Having conquered territories, he would generally allow local cultures and customs to continue – he even adopted many Persian mannerisms himself – and thus built up a network of imperial allies. But he was the glue holding his conquests together. After his death in 323 BCE, the empire steadily collapsed as other empires and states began to eat away at the Macedonian territories. In the 2nd century BCE, Greece itself would succumb to what would be the crowning power of the ancient world – Rome.

THE ROMAN WAR MACHINE

The history of Rome, and the empire that it forged, covers a period of more than 1,000 years, so a close review of its history is beyond the scope of this book. What is clear, however, is that Rome would not have grown from a small city-state into one of history's largest and most enduring empires without the capabilities of an exceptional army. This army evolved as a citizen force during the 6th century BCE, conscripted to meet the needs of specific campaigns.

It took several centuries and numerous reforms to make it into the consistently battle-winning force it became.

Between the 5th and the 3rd centuries BCE, Rome was locked within an endless sequence of wars, as it steadily expanded its power within the Italian mainland and then further afield into Greece around the edges of the Mediterranean. Looking back at the tapestry of battles Rome fought during this era, we are struck as much by the defeats as by the victories. In 390 BCE, for example, Celtic forces from northern Europe – known for fighting in a frenzied manner that the formalized Roman tactics of this time found hard to counter – defeated a Roman army at Allia then advanced on Rome, occupying much of the city; only payment of a large tribute encouraged them to leave. During the Battle of the Caudine Forks in 321 BCE, the Roman Army was nearly wiped out in a mountainous past by a Samnite ambush. In 218 BCE, during the Punic Wars between Rome and Carthage (264–146 BCE), the bold Carthaginian leader Hannibal marched an army from Spain, through Gaul, crossed the Alps, and ultimately ran wild in northern Italy for a period of some 15 years. During this time, he inflicted numerous defeats upon the Romans: at Trebia (218 BCE), Lake Trasimene (217 BCE) and, most grievously, at Cannae in 216 BCE – with Roman losses of 50,000 men, it was the worst defeat in Roman military history.

Yet the Roman Army was an adaptable and resilient entity, rebounding from defeats with equal and greater victories and learning from its mistakes in the hands of new generations of commanders. As it went into the 2nd century BCE, the Roman Army had been through several important periods of reform that strengthened its discipline and fighting prowess. Its legions – potent formations each numbering some 4,500–5,000 men – contained a mixture of veterans and new recruits, the ranks intelligently ordered so that the wiser heads could support the younger warriors. Legions were ordered by cohort, maniple and century sub-divisions, and each Roman legion was mirrored by an allied legion; two Roman and two allied legions together formed a consular army, so called because it was led by one of Rome's two consuls (the highest elected officials in the Roman state). Command of this army on campaign rotated between the two men on a daily basis, although this rule was sometimes suspended.

Hannibal (247–182 bce)

Son of the great Carthaginian general Hamilcar Barca, Hannibal grew up dedicated to avenging the defeat inflicted upon Carthage during the First Punic War (246–41 bce), in which his father served. In 218 bce, he famously led his army over the Alps and into Italy, losing many thousands of men to the brutal march. But Hannibal handled his multi-ethnic army brilliantly, tactically optimizing the various national strengths within his manpower. The major victories he took over the Romans between 218 and 216 bce led to his control over much of Italy for more than a decade, the Carthaginian leader being known especially for his skilful and coordinated manoeuvring of both infantry and cavalry. Ultimately, however, Hannibal was less adept at fighting long wars of attrition, and he was eventually forced to abandon his Italian conquests and suffer under Roman victories in North Africa. After 195 bce, Hannibal went into exile, and committed suicide by poisoning at some point in 183–81 bce in Bithynia, opting for death rather than surrender to the Romans who were still pursuing him.

A notable tactical feature of the Republican Roman army at war was the spaced checkerboard-like *quincunx* formation of individual maniples (each containing 120 or 60 men, depending on the type of troops). Each maniple acted like its own small phalanx, making the Roman Army tactically adaptable and manoeuvrable, closing up or opening its ranks and lines as required and better able to handle rough terrain. The bulk of the soldiers were armed with two *pilum* throwing javelins, launched into enemy ranks just before the main clash, and a broad-bladed *gladius* short sword, ideal for close-quarters fighting, at which the Romans excelled through hard, consistent training.

The professionalism, high morale and formidable stoicism of the Roman Army, combined with excellence in logistics and canny imperial politics, bought Rome an empire that stretched, by *c.*50 BCE, from the North Sea to the shores of the eastern Mediterranean. The conquests, which included all of Gaul (most of modern-day France and Belgium), were added to the empire by the Roman proconsul Julius Caesar and his armies in 58–50 BCE. During the 1st century BCE, however, the empire to a large extent turned upon itself in a series of civil wars as rival factions clamoured for power, the situation made worse by the fact that Roman legions often laid their loyalty at the feet of their commander, rather than the Roman state per se. The civil war claimed many great leaders, including Caesar, who was assassinated in 44 BCE. The ultimate winner was Octavian, the great-nephew of Caesar. On 2 September 31 BCE, Octavian's 400-strong fleet or warships routed those of his former ally Anthony, who was now allied and married to Queen Cleopatra of Egypt, at the Battle of Actium, off the coast of western Greece.

Octavian's victory at Actium brought him unchallenged power in Rome; Rome now became an Empire rather than a republic, and Octavian took the title of Emperor Augustus (r. 27 BCE–14 CE), ushering in the *c.*200 years of the *pax romana*. Although this was a period of stability in terms of central Roman governance, war bubbled away with varying levels of intensity throughout the reign of Augustus and that of subsequent emperors during the 1st and 2nd centuries CE. Rome's imperial forces were kept endlessly busy protecting frontier regions, a service that Augustus improved by settling demobilized veterans throughout the borderlands of the empire, where they could both improve the imperial economy through farming activities and also act as an *in situ* reserve should Roman territories come under threat or attack.

The regular legionary army, which wavered in strength between *c.*300,000 and 500,000 between the 1st and 5th centuries CE, was a small force to police such a vast territory, which reached its height under the Emperor Trajan (r. 98–117), by which time it incorporated almost all the land between Northern Britain and the Persian Gulf. It achieved this feat of territorial management through emplacing troops in chains of permanent camps and blockhouses (*castella*) along the frontier regions, as well as through an increasingly heavy use of non-Roman auxiliaries – during Augustus' reign alone, the total Roman army included some 150,000 auxiliary troops. The shifting loyalties of such soldiers were demonstrated in sobering fashion in September 9 CE in the Teutoburg Forest in Germany, where three Roman legions were massacred after a Cherusci tribe army, led by Arminius, turned on their former allies.

Despite such localized disasters, during the 1st and 2nd centuries CE Roman rule reigned supreme. Britain was incorporated into the empire following its invasion in 43 CE by Emperor Claudius and the subsequent rebellion of the British Celts, led by Queen Boudicca of the Iceni Tribe in 60–1 CE, was eventually crushed. The Emperor Trajan subjugated the wilful Dacians during his campaigns of 101–06 CE and then dominated the Parthians, Rome's long-standing foe to the east, between 115 and 117 CE. Trajan's successor Hadrian (r. 117–38 CE) was similarly militaristic in outlook, and made further consolidations of the empire, including the construction of his famous wall across the far north of Britain, to keep at bay the fearsome Celtic tribes to the north.

The long, slow decline of Rome began in the 3rd century, as Rome itself progressively lost centralized authority over the empire, which became divided in the 4th century between Eastern and Western empires, the former centred upon Constantinople/ Byzantium. The Western Roman Empire re-formed its military machine frequently to hold back the tide of threats on its periphery, especially to the north, whence hailed a variety of warrior tribes, which had an increasingly predatory attitude towards a weakening Rome.

After a major defeat at the hands of the Ostrogoths and Visigoths at Adrianople (present-day Edirne, western Turkey) in August 378, one notable change was that the Roman Army became increasingly cavalry focused, with up to 25 per cent of its entire

 Roman ballistae *were an early form of artillery. They used torsion springs to fire either rocks or bolts over considerable distances – more than 300 m (328 yd) – and were typically used in either siege warfare, naval warfare or against large masses of enemy troops.*

army becoming mounted troops; the Romans were now leaning towards mobility and manoeuvre rather than the stoic press of the infantry. Through these and similar innovations, the Roman Army remained a truly formidable force in the West until the very end of days, capable of winning big battles. In 394, for example, Emperor Theodosius (r. 379–92) – the last of the emperors to rule over both halves of the empire – wiped out a Frankish army led by Arbogast during the Battle of the Frigidus on the Isonzo River in Italy. It is notable, however, that the Roman ranks included 20,000 Gothic allies, led by the Vandal general Stilicho, one of the great 'Roman' generals of the last century of empire. At Chalons, north-east France, in 451, the Roman general Aetius inflicted a similar heavy defeat upon the terrifying band of warriors led by Attila the Hun (r. 434–53), who preyed on both the Eastern and Western Empires between 441 and 453 with devastating effect, albeit without taking Rome itself.

Yet in 455, Rome was ultimately taken and sacked by a Vandal army. The vulnerability of Rome was by now understood, for it had previously been sacked in 410 by the Visigoths under Alaric. (Rome was actually no longer the capital of the Western Roman Empire – it had migrated to Mediolanum in 286 and Ravenna in 402 – but the city still held a special status throughout the West.) Rome would be sacked twice more in the 6th century, by the Ostrogoths, but by this stage the authority of the Western Roman Empire was largely nominal; as we shall see in the next chapter, the power of the Eastern, or Byzantine, Empire, was only just beginning.

WARFARE IN INDIA AND CHINA

Although the Romans undoubtedly built one of the most powerful and effective of the ancient armies, they were not alone in ownership of sophisticated imperial forces. Half a world away, both the Chinese and the Indians wielded major armies during the 2nd and

1st millennia BCE. Much as with the Romans, these armies were the instruments of empire, used both to acquire new territories and to defend those territories from the inevitable aggression or pushback of external powers.

China's earliest armies were centred around chariot-borne mobile troops, foot soldiers and archers. A formative influence over the development of the ancient Chinese armed forces was Emperor Qin Shi Huang (r. 247–21 BCE), the first emperor of a unified China. He did military history a service by ordering the production of the 'Terracotta Army', a vast host of terracotta funerary figures that includes more than 8,000 foot soldiers, 130 chariots and 150 cavalry horses. Many of the foot soldiers are armed with advanced crossbows, powerful enough to penetrate plate armour. These weapons, introduced by the Chinese centuries before they became commonplace in the West, were an integral part of the 'combined arms' approach adopted by the Chinese military. A regiment of soldiers, totalling about 1,000 troops, would contain a mix of heavy armoured infantry, light infantry (which included crossbowmen, archers and spearmen), cavalry and chariots, fighting together in a coordinated and supportive fashion.

Qin Shi Huang seems to have been especially invested in increasing the numbers of crossbowmen in the ranks, giving his troops a distinct firepower advantage. He did not introduce the weapon – at the earlier Battle of Guai Ling in 341 BCE, for example, the forces of the state of Wei were utterly defeated when they were drawn into a mass crossbow ambush by the Qi army.

The Chinese way of war stayed fairly constant well into the medieval period. Battles were fought on a huge scale, showing that tactical principles employed were capable of being scaled up. For instance, although we do not have accurate orders of battle for the clash at Changping in 260 BCE between the Qin and the Zhao, the reported figure of 400,000 Zhao dead, though likely fictitious, indicates combat on a scale equal to anything in the Western hemisphere.

The Chinese imperial armies, in a familiar story, met their match facing opponents from outside the empire who fought with very tactical different styles. The two major dynasties of ancient China – the Qin dynasty (221–06 BCE) and the succeeding Han dynasty (206 BCE–220 CE) – both had large empires to maintain, with all the economic and military expenditure that entailed. Early on in the Han dynasty, an invasion by Xiongnu nomads from Mongolia dealt the Han some wincing defeats, the Chinese ranks struggling to contend with the enemy's flowing mounted archers. At the other end of its dynastic lifespan, the Han took a final crushing defeat at the Battle of Red Cliffs in 208 CE, Cao Cao, the Han leader, being drawn reluctantly into a naval battle – not a Han strength – on the Yangtze River by southern warlords, who destroyed the Han fleet with fire arrows and fireships.

The Terracotta Army provides an unrivalled insight into the Chinese military of the late 3rd century BCE. The individual faces of each warrior have led some to consider that each figure is based on a real human.

Looking across to India, our insight into ancient warfare in the Indian subcontinent is hampered by a paucity of historical sources, but we have sufficient information to construct a partial picture. One of the earliest sources, although mythical in theme, is the Sanskrit epic *Mahabharata*, which was likely composed in the 4th century BCE, albeit based on older traditions. From such sources, we can gather that by the 1st millennium BCE Indian rulers had developed significant standing armies, centred around large numbers of foot soldiers who were armed primarily with bows and swords and supported by chariots that were characteristically manned by the warrior nobility. War elephants provided a vehicle to shock and smash enemy ranks and field fortifications, although the actual effectiveness of the great creatures on the battlefield was limited.

We can also draw upon the *Arthashastra* ('Manual of Politics'), attributed to Kautilya. This is a work of statecraft that was composed in the 3rd century BCE and that contains three individual books dedicated to explaining the Indian military system. Interestingly, the *Arthashastra* explains the activities of war as far wider than mere battlefield clashes; propaganda, spying, disinformation, morale building and many other more subtle factors have roles to play in the eventual victory or defeat.

Kautilya was an official within the court of Chandragupta Maurya (r. 321–298 BCE), the founder of the Maurya Empire. Chandragupta, influenced by Alexander the Great, and his successors built an extensive empire across northern India and much of South Asia. The wars of this time could be extraordinarily cruel, hinting at elements of 'total war' we would see later in history. During the reign of Emperor Ashoka (r. *c.*268–*c.*32 BCE), for example, Mauryan forces invaded and devastated the state of Kalinga in *c.*262 BCE, the Kalingans having refused Mauryan authority. To reinforce the subjugation, Ashoka unleashed the murder of some 100,000 Kalingans. In fact, such was the horror of this spectacle that Ashoka subsequently adopted Buddhism and became an advocate of peaceful state policies. The Mauryan Empire collapsed in the 2nd century BCE.

The other great Indian empire of the ancient period was the Gupta Empire, founded by Chandragupta I (r. 319–50) – the name was an intentional nod to the Mauryan founder – and expanded significantly by his son Samudragupta (r. 350–75), a formidable warrior. This empire folded in the 6th century under the invasion of the White Huns – just one of many Central Asian peoples who had been probing and invading northern India since the 1st century CE.

Throughout our exploration of ancient wars and armies in this chapter, we frequently return to rhythms of imperial expansion then contraction then collapse. It is evident that empires, and the armies within them, have a finite lifespan. The ancient armies were just part of an overall social, cultural, economic and political package; fighting capabilities alone could not guarantee perpetual security of a state or empire. Furthermore, just as old empires consolidated their hold, new empires were rising on the horizon. As we shall see in the next chapter, the ebb and flow of power was constant, and the ways of making war itself would undergo some profound changes.

CHAPTER 2
THE MIDDLE AGES

The Middle Ages (c.500–1500), seen globally, was a time of extraordinary chaos. Wars were frequent and bloody, cynical and fanatical, fought for motives ranging from political manoeuvring to extremes of religious faith. By the end of the period, however, warfare itself was beginning the shift to modernity.

What we today refer to as the 'Middle Ages' is largely applied to a Western-centric view of history, bracketed between the collapse of the Western Roman Empire in the 5th century and the fall of Constantinople to the Ottoman Turks in 1453. This period of roughly 1,000 years, however, is truly significant in the global history of warfare. Not only do we see signal changes in the nature of the way wars were fought – although ancient modes of combat persisted – but we also see military campaigns literally reshaping the social and ideological fabric of the world. These events include the campaigns of the Franks, Vikings and Normans, the electrifying expansion of Islam, the forging of the Mongol Empire, the ascent of the samurai, the rise and fall of the Byzantine Empire, and the interminably exhausting religious wars in Western Europe. A citizen of this era truly lived in precarious, formative times.

WAR-MAKING IN THE MIDDLE AGES

We should first set the compass to orientate ourselves through some of the key military themes of this period. There was much that was familiar from earlier times – wars were still fought by

This portion of the Bayeux Tapestry shows English infantry battling Norman cavalry in the 11th century. The battleaxe at front was a powerful tool for felling horses; the tapestry elsewhere shows horses brought down by single strikes to the head.

a combination of foot soldiers and cavalry. But, crucially, the cavalry now became psychologically and practically the arm of decision, the elite, and the weight of almost all armies. Tactical emphasis was primarily on mounted manoeuvre by cavalry troops (although cavalry would frequently dismount to fight), a focus socially reinforced by the often privileged origins of the cavalry, particularly in the West – this was the era of the chivalric knight, fighting from horseback with lance and sword in gleaming armour. There was some considerable diversity within the cavalry, especially when viewed internationally. In the Middle East and Central Asia, cavalry tended to be light, fast and armed with the bow, while in the West the cavalryman tended towards heavier armour and hand-to-hand fighting at close quarters (allowing for many exceptions to this general picture).

Foot soldiers, despite on many occasions being handled either chaotically or unimaginatively, still had a crucial role to play in warfare, not least in siege warfare. For the Middle Ages was an era of fortifications, scattered geographically in huge numbers and with ever-increasing defensive capabilities as kings, nobles and warlords sought to project and consolidate their power across restless territories or threatened frontiers. Besieging these structures became not only an act of endurance, but also an engineering enterprise of great sophistication, characterized by the use of advanced siege engines such as counterweight trebuchets and, from the 14th century, gunpowder cannon. On the open battlefield, foot soldiers steadily adapted to the reality of the cavalry charge. Crossbows and bows, of various types, provided effective stand-off attrition against even the most elite cavalry forces, while disciplined handling of pikes, halberds and other pole arms presented a near-impenetrable barrier to the horsemen. In the last century of the Middle Ages, we also see the first handheld firearms make their crude entrance, as did mobile battlefield artillery. Nobles might not have perceived it at that time, but these gunpowder weapons would eventually become the deciding instruments of warfare.

In the war at sea, there were also changes. Although oar-powered galleys still ruled naval warfare for much of this period, sail steadily took precedence, at first with single-masted vessels, often working as auxiliary power to banks of oars, but by the 14th and 15th centuries expressed in great three- or four-masted carracks, equipped with deck-mounted cannon and high castles fore and aft, which served as platforms for archers and maritime infantry. With the emergence of such vessels, a smoky battlefield sun rose on the era of global maritime warfare.

So the Middle Ages were a time of steady transformation in the art of war. Much of this transformation came later in the period, however; a large portion of the medieval age is simply characterized by grinding and unimaginative brutality, punctuated by occasional acts of military discipline, intelligence and even brilliance.

WESTERN EUROPE IN THE EARLY MIDDLE AGES

What historians refer to as the 'Early Middle Ages' (5th–10th centuries) have been popularly labelled the 'Dark Ages'. Although this term is now regarded as clunkily inaccurate, it nevertheless gives a sense of the chaos and violence that pervaded Europe in the aftermath of the collapse of the Western Roman Empire. Numberless local and regional wars were fought as monarchs, nobles, warlords, migrants and raiders fought for power and land. Taking a very broad brush, however, by c.600 Western Europe was roughly divided into: the Anglo-Saxon kingdoms and the Celtic territories of Britain; the kingdom of the Franks (most of modern France); an Iberian Peninsula dominated by the Visigoths; various Germanic and Slavic tribes east of the Rhine; the Pannonian Avars in Central and Eastern Europe; Italy controlled mostly by the Lombards; and the Byzantine Empire (Eastern Roman Empire),

 Knightly cavalry warfare appeared noble in art, but was brutal in reality. Knights often met their end when dismounted, finished off by infantry armed with daggers and hammers.

which incorporated the Balkans, Anatolia, Palestine and much of the Mediterranean rim. These entities were in a state of constant flux, either aggressively conducting offensive campaigns to expand their powerbase, or responding to the constant depredations of raiders or invaders.

By the 8th century, the Franks undoubtedly held the commanding position in Western Europe, having extended their empire in Gaul through a series of victories over the Saxons, Danes, Visigoths, Avars, Lombards and others. At its height, this empire incorporated France, Germany, Italy, the Iberian Peninsula and much of the Balkans. The Franks also secured a critical victory at Poitiers in *c.*732, when Charles Martel defeated Muslim forces led by Abd al-Rahman, the governor of Muslim Spain.

The Franks accomplished this imperial surge with an effective army, led by some impressive commanders. Of all these leaders, historical pole position goes to Charlemagne, King of the Franks from 768–814 and, from 800, 'Emperor of the Romans', a title bestowed by Pope Leo III. A true warrior monarch, Charlemagne demonstrated consistent competence in his campaigns against the Lombards, Saxons, Avars and Slavs. By the end of his rule, the Frankish army had largely become a cavalry force, the mounted troops fighting with lance, spear and sword and protected by a mail coat, or 'byrnie'. The infantry consisted of part-time levies of free men, those wealthy enough to afford basic armour and a weapon. The primary virtue of the Frankish infantry was their disciplined formations; at Poitiers, the wheeling Muslim cavalry were held off and beaten largely by tight-packed Frankish infantry squares.

 Mail armour was made from numerous interlinked iron rings, each ring closed by welding or riveting. Mail was especially protective against slashes and broad blade penetrations, but gave less protection against heavy impact injuries.

Saddle and Stirrup

Two of the most important technological developments in the history of cavalry warfare were the saddle and the stirrup. Early saddles emerge around 700 BCE in Assyria, although more solid frame saddles appear to date from about 200 years later. Around 200 BCE, solid-tree saddles were developed. These featured a wooden frame that both protected the horse's back from impact and pressure and also made the ride more comfortable for the user. During the Middle Ages, such saddles were further refined, improved designs largely driven by the need for better support for heavy armoured warriors. With their high cantles and pommels, these saddles reduced the risk of cavalry being dismounted from their horses in combat, especially under the impact of a lance (either delivered or suffered).

Allied to the development of the saddle was that of the stirrup. Stirrups are first seen in India in the 2nd century BCE, and spread through China and Central Asia, reaching Europe around the 9th century. Stirrups not only provided a more solid platform for fighting with the lance, but they also gave the mounted warrior improved balance, enabling him to fight more dynamically from horseback with sword and spear.

The Vikings – that much-mythologized sea-faring people of medieval Scandinavia – offer an illuminating contrast to the army of the Franks. As well as being sophisticated explorers and traders (qualities often overlooked), whose voyages took them as far as North America and India, the Vikings were militarily a raider culture, preying mostly on coastal settlements but also making deep inland incursions, depending on the waterways. The main instrument of Viking foreign policy was the longship, a sleek vessel powered primarily by oars but also a single sail. The longship was fast and robust, able to make open-ocean journeys, but with a shallow draft that was perfect for executing amphibious landings or traversing shallow rivers. A double prow meant that the ship could be beached or extracted from the landing site with equal speed and ease. It was also light enough that, if required, the crew could even shoulder the boat and carry it for short distances across land.

The Viking warriors themselves were known for their ferocity in battle, fighting with brutal commitment using double-edged swords, spears, battle axes (the two-handed Dane axe could split a man in two) and bows. Yet they also exercised discipline, composing battlefield formations using archers, shield walls, light skirmishers and heavy infantry to fight more organized enemies. During the 8th and 9th centuries in particular, the Vikings were the terror of Europe. At first, they raided mostly for plunder. The sack of the Lindisfarne monastery on the north-east coast of England in 793 is a particularly famous example of a Viking assault, one that began the relentless Viking campaign against the Anglo-Saxons. However, over time, the scale of Viking targets and ambitions became ever greater, and the raiders turned to settlers in many areas. During the 9th century, Vikings besieged or attacked Utrecht, Antwerp, Paris and Constantinople. In Britain, Danish Vikings invaded and occupied the kingdoms of Northumbria, Mercia and East Anglia between 865 and 890; the Danish King Guthrum's attempt to incorporate Wessex in 878 was repelled by King Alfred's victory at the Battle of Edington in May 878, and thereafter England was divided between Anglo-Saxon territories and the Viking Danelaw.

Viking control over England ebbed and flowed during the 9th and 10th centuries, but they were becoming established elsewhere. Most significantly, in 911 the Frankish King Charles III of West Francia (r. 893–929) gave the Viking ruler Rollo territories in northern France, in return for guarantees that France would be spared further Viking raids. These Viking settlers would become the Normans, one of the most militarily successful warrior peoples of the medieval period. The crowning Norman achievement came on 14 October 1066, when William of Normandy – aka William the Conqueror – defeated the army of King Harold Godwinson (r. 1066) at the Battle of Hastings in southern England. This victory brought England under Norman rule – a rule that William enforced with a brutal efficiency, quashing rebellions and resistance throughout the land.

BYZANTINE EMPIRE

Although the Western Roman Empire collapsed in the 5th century, its imperial heir, what we today mainly refer to as the Byzantine Empire, would endure for a thousand troubled years. Its capital, Constantinople (also Byzantium), stood as a luminous cultural beacon in Eastern Europe. Yet the Byzantine Empire came to straddle that most dangerous of geographical, political and religious fault lines, between the Christian West and the Islamic East, and thus its fate was perhaps predestined.

The longevity of the Byzantine Empire can to a large degree be laid at the door of its military. The Byzantine army utilized all that was best from Roman military practice, while adapting and innovating according to the times. Under the Emperor Justinian (r. 527–65), the army consisted of about 300,000–350,000 troops, but for much of the empire's history the standing army numbered 120,000–150,000; as with the Roman army, this was not a huge force to police the extent of a widely spread empire. The compensation was the army's professionalism and organization. It was recruited by a process of universal military conscription, and divided between district garrisons scattered throughout the empire (the districts were called themes, and there were about 30 of them

✳ *This 13th-century artwork depicts the violent clash between Byzantine and Muslim Arab cavalry at the battle of Lalakaon (3 September 863). This engagement in what is today northern Turkey ended in a Byzantine victory.*

by the 10th century). The Byzantine infantry was divided into light and heavy types, the former clothed in padded leather jackets and steel helmets, and armed with javelin or bow and a short sword. Heavy infantry, called scutari, donned extensive armour, including mail shirts, gauntlets and greaves. The most imposing expression of the Byzantine cavalry was the cataphracts, heavy armoured horsemen who fought with bow, broadsword, long lance, axe and dagger. Light cavalry provided skirmishing, reconnaissance, scouting and screening duties.

Greek Fire

Unique to the Byzantines, Greek Fire was an intriguing incendiary formula in the medieval world, producing what was a progenitor of the modern flamethrower. The exact composition of the combustible compound is lost to history – likely constituents include naptha and quicklime, with pine resin, sulphur or calcium phosphide being possible additives. What we know, however, is that it burned with consuming intensity, even in contact with water. In a naval context, it was projected from a pressurized metal nozzle called a *siphon*, the pressure provided by a large set of bellows; there was a handheld version, and Greek Fire was also placed into ceramic hand grenades. The *siphon* had a maximum range of about 15 cm (16 yards).

On the battlefield, the Byzantine army typically presented its *scutari* in deep ranks in the centre, flanked or fronted by light infantry, with the *cataphracts* on the outer flanks and also positioned as a mobile reserve to the rear. The light infantry were spread about as screening forces. In action, depending on the commander, this army could operate with a reasonable degree of flexibility, responding to the bespoke challenges of the enemy and the terrain. The Byzantines also deployed an effective supply and baggage train, meaning that they could undertake long-distance operations, and had excellent systems of signalling and command. The army also possessed a respected maritime counterpart in the Byzantine navy, consisting of a fleet of light galleys, each with a complement of 200–300 men (combat rowers and marines), plus heavy warships equipped with on-deck siege engines (useful for tackling coastal fortifications) and also Greek Fire ejectors.

During the 6th and 7th centuries, the Byzantine emperors used their armies in bold campaigns to both east and west. Emperor Justinian, largely through the talents of his exceptional general Belisarius, reclaimed major territories around the Mediterranean, and took Italy from the Goths. Belisarius also inflicted a major defeat upon the Persians, a perennial adversary of Byzantium, at the Battle of Dara (530), the Byzantines making good use of allied Hun archers to impose heavy casualties upon Persian heavy cavalry every time they surged forwards. Persia gained ascendancy in the late 6th and early 7th centuries, but at the 11-hour Battle of Nineveh (12 December 627) Emperor Heraclius (r. 610–41) took an impressive victory. Demonstrating that this was the age in which some rulers truly did lead from the front, Heraclius personally killed three Persian generals in single combat.

The victory at Nineveh, as impressive as it was, did not ensure, however, that Constantinople sailed into a future of peace and stability. For further south, a new enemy was arising – one that would change the religious and cultural map of the world to the same extent as Christianity.

ISLAM AND THE CRUSADES

In 610, in a remote cave in southern Arabia, the Prophet Muhammad is said to have received a revelation from God – one

ΓΕΡΟϹΗΙΤΩΝΟΙ
ΙΕΝΑΝΤΙΟΝ:

ΙϹΟΤΟΥΝΑΥΗ

ΗΜΙΜΗΧΑΗΛΟΑΡΧΗ
ΤΙΓΟϹΤΗϹΔΥΝΑΜΕ
ΥΚΑΙΗΛΘΟΝΤΟΥ
ϹΧΥΕΕϹΕ:

A Byzantine soldier depicted in a medieval fresco. His torso is protected by lamellar armour made from small rectangular plates of metal set in horizontal rows on a rawhide background.

that became the religion of Islam. Converts flocked to the faith, and by 622 the first Muslim state had been formed, accompanied by the energetic new Muslim armies. Over the next extraordinary century, Muslim armies, the ranks continually swelled by new believers, carved out an Islamic empire that included the Arabian Peninsula, Syria, Palestine, the territories of the Persian empire, Afghanistan, Egypt and most of North Africa, and even the Iberian Peninsula, with deep incursions into what is today central France. They even laid siege to Constantinople in 717–18 – the Byzantine Empire was one of tallest obstacles to expansion – although the city walls, the defensive talents of Emperor Leo III, the strengths of the Byzantine navy, plus the effects of disease and storm weather eventually stopped and reversed the Muslim effort there.

The story of this expansion has a complexity beyond the telling of this book, but there are some key points. The first is that although there is no doubting the growing military skill and confidence of the Islamic armies, their growth was certainly assisted by the exhaustion of some of its enemies, particular the Byzantines and the Persians, who had been slugging it out with each other for a century. Second, the nature of the Islamic armies, both militarily and politically, changed profoundly as the centuries wore on. The question of who would rightfully take the title of 'caliph' (the successors of Muhammed) produced the first Muslim caliphate (an Islamic political-religious state) in 632: the Rashidun Caliphate (632–61). This was followed by the more enduring Umayyad Caliphate (661–750), and then the Abbasid Caliphate (750–1258). It also produced the theological split between what became the Sunni and Shia branches of Islam, fostering rival caliphs and creating internal conflict within Islam that restrained further expansion, and that exists to this day.

Nevertheless, the early Islamic armies would not have been able to make such an impressive land grab had they not demonstrated military talent. Muslim light cavalry was especially strong, making flanking or encircling attacks with blurring speed and dexterity, striking with lances, swords and bows. Infantry would make repeated attacks and withdrawals to weaken their enemies' strength, before building up to a concerted charge. Such tactics, delivered with absolute religious fervour, often left more traditional opponents bewildered and outmanoeuvered.

Over time, the composition of the Islamic armies changed significantly. As Muslim rulers built their own states, a large portion of the fighting armies was composed of Muslim Turkish slave warriors, heavily recruited from Central Asia. These were excellent soldiers, noted for their horseback archery but also for their ferocity in close-quarters combat. During the 10th and 11th centuries, the Turkish element of Islam grew to be a dominant imperial presence in its own right, first with the Ghazni Turks and then with the Seljuk Turks, who ruled over large expanses of territory in Central Asia and the Middle East from the 11th to the 14th centuries. Thus it is important that when we talk about the 'Islamic' empire, we do not think of it as a single monolithic entity; it was as diverse and fractured as the Christian world.

In 1071, the Byzantine emperor Romanus IV Diogenes (r. 1068–71) led an army out against the Seljuk Turks, who had been attacking Byzantine territories in Armenia and Anatolia. At Manzikert (now Malazgirt in Armenia), the Turkish forces under their seminal commander Alp Arslan utterly routed the Byzantines. It was in part this defeat that led to what we now refer as the Crusades, two centuries of war-making by the Christian West against the Islamic empire.

The Crusades began in earnest in 1095, when Pope Urban II, responding to a call for help from Byzantine emperor Alexios I Komnenos (r. 1081–1118), called upon the knights of Christendom to engage in a military pilgrimage to the Holy Land. The ultimate goal was to take back the Holy Land and the city of Jerusalem from the Muslims, who had held it now for some 400 years. Europe's nobility, and thousands of lesser warriors, responded to the call, tempted by both the potential material gains and also by the religious indulgence (forgiveness of sins) promised by the Church to those who embarked on the campaign.

The exact number of the Crusades, and the timescale over which they happened, are open to historical debate. Conventionally, there were nine crusades between 1095 and 1291, but if we include the wider context of the Crusades – particularly actions against pagan peoples in the far north of Europe and conflicts with the Ottomans – then some see crusading activities going on until the 16th century. The First Crusade (1095–99) was arguably the campaign most in alignment with the overarching religious and territorial goals of the Crusades in general. After an arduous and harrowing 4,000 km (2,500-mile) overland journey from Europe to the Middle East, which nearly ended in disaster under the attacks of Seljuk Turks in Anatolia (this part of the journey would be a perennial hazard for future crusaders), the weary Europeans eventually recovered Antioch and Jerusalem.

This triumph laid the groundwork for the establishment of the 'Crusader States' in the Levant – the Kingdom of Jerusalem, the Principality of Antioch, the County of Tripoli and the County of Edessa. The subsequent eight crusades, launched to make further incursions against the Muslims or to reclaim territories snatched back by Islamic counter-strikes, increasingly lost their moral and political compass. The ignominious Fourth Crusade (1202–04), for example, saw the crusader army not only capture and sack the Hungarian Christian city of Zara in 1202, as a repayment for Venetian invasion shipping, but then go on to besiege and sack Constantinople itself in 1203–04, unleashing a horrifying massacre in the aftermath.

Back in Europe, the launch of crusades was often accompanied by cruel diversions to murder local Jews, as if in some grotesque warm-up activity. Political manoeuvring also meant that the Crusader States fought one another, as did Muslim states, and Muslims and Christians also formed opportunistic alliances against common enemies. Progressively, the Crusaders dropped their grip in the Middle East and in 1291, with the destruction of Acre by the Turkish Mamluks, the Christians let slip their last foothold in the Holy Land. In balance, however, between the 11th century and the 15th century the 'Reconquista' saw the Muslim rulers of the Iberian Peninsula progressively squeezed out by Christian expansion, Granada falling after an eight-month siege on New Year's Day, 1492.

THE MONGOLS

Today, it is perhaps hard to appreciate the impact of the Mongols not just on the territories from which they originated – modern-day eastern Mongolia and Manchuria – but also on much of the world during the 13th century. Quite simply, Mongol military conquests created the largest contiguous land empire in history, one that reached from Korea across to Eastern Europe, with invasions into Austria.

The Mongol army was, in itself, not particularly large – perhaps around 105,000 men at the beginning of the 13th century. It was logically divided into units of ten-man squads (*arvan*), 100-man companies (*zuun*), 1,000-man battalions (*mingghan*) and 10,000 men divisions (*tumens*), plus a sizeable imperial guard for the khan (ruler) and senior generals. The scale of the army, however, was enhanced by the acquisition of allies, especially Turkish, Arab and Chinese warriors.

Mongol rulers tended to issue a simple option as they advanced on a new territory: resist and be crushed in the most merciless fashion, or bend the knee and be spared. The Mongol army was almost entirely a mounted force, who fought from the saddle with composite bows, hand axes, lances and curved sabres. In battle, the cavalry would use psychology as much as tactics to win the field; they were particularly known for feigned retreats in order to break open enemy ranks. We see this in the Battle of Liegnitz (south-west Poland) on 9 April 1241. In this battle, the Mongols appeared to retreat before a push from German, Polish and Teutonic cavalry, only to then turn back, encircle and destroy the charge. In terms of operational ability, being a mounted army meant that the Mongols could campaign over extremely long distances, not least because they lived almost entirely off the land through which they travelled and plundered.

At the beginning of their conquests, the Mongols were not naturally an army talented in siege warfare. Recognizing this deficit, however, they soon acquired the skills and related technologies from the Chinese; indeed, Chinese siege engineers accompanied the Mongols on campaign. Consequently, the Mongols became adept at bringing down even the most defiant of fortresses. In January–February 1258, for example, Hulagu, the Mongol khan of Persia (the Mongol Empire was divided into distinct khanates) destroyed an Abbasid army outside Baghdad and then proceeded to besiege and take the city itself, smashing breaches in the walls with huge catapults. When the city surrendered on 10 February, it was characteristically subjected to the most extreme levels of massacre and torture; Hulagu is said to have abandoned the city because he could no longer bear the stench of decaying corpses.

The Mongols benefited from leaders of ruthless brilliance. Of supreme infamy is Genghis Khan (r. 1206–27), known as much for his conquests as for his appetite for blood. Genghis conquered huge swathes of Asia and northern China, and his offensive momentum continued under his son Ögedei (r. 1229–41), who

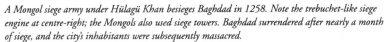

A Mongol siege army under Hülagü Khan besieges Baghdad in 1258. Note the trebuchet-like siege engine at centre-right; the Mongols also used siege towers. Baghdad surrendered after nearly a month of siege, and the city's inhabitants were subsequently massacred.

took the Mongols to Eastern Europe and the Mediterranean, and his grandson Kublai Khan (r. 1260–94), who furthered advanced into China. Another great name in the Mongol pantheon of leaders is Timur (r. 1370–1405), actually a Turkic Uzbek who claimed descent from Genghis Khan and who campaigned extensively in Persia, India, Syria and Anatolia. Like his claimed distant forebears, Timur was capable of daunting cruelty. After the revolt of the city of Isfahan in 1387, he instructed his 70,000-man army to go to the city and bring back a single human head each; the heads were used to create a pyramid. Timur was nevertheless a diligent and conscientious military commander, who led from the front and had a special interest in logistics, the mark of every judicious commander.

Eventually, time wore down the Mongol Empire. Divided into separate khanates, its power and cohesion were whittled away, although the last of the khanates did not disappear until the 17th century.

CHINA

As indicated by the account of the Mongols, the military history of China during the Middle Ages was intimately bound up with that of aggressive neighbours. But China itself, among the most advanced civilizations on earth at this time, also had its own expeditionary focus. During the 7th century, the army of the Tang dynasty fought distant, prolonged campaigns in Tibet and Central Asia, aided by Emperor Xuanzong's (r. 712–56) introduction of long-term service, rather than replacing conscripted soldiers every three years.

By 742, the army numbered about 500,000 men. The Tang also invested heavily in the navy, building a spectrum of fighting vessels for use in both open-water and littoral combat.

The Tang dynasty progressively weakened in the 9th and 10th century, and was replaced by the Song dynasty in 960, which at its peak had some 1 million men under arms. Although imperial suspicion of generals severely weakened the Song command efficiency, this era (the dynasty lasted until 1279) was generally a time in which military science and technology were encouraged. Crossbow designs were improved to increase range and penetration; gunpowder weapons – of which the Chinese were historical pioneers – were developed, including rockets, grenades and 'fire lances' (a handheld weapon rather like a cross between a flamethrower and a shotgun); anti-cavalry tactics were improved; and large troop-carrying ships were produced. Despite the size of the army, and the weapons therein, the Song dynasty could not prevent its eventual collapse under the expansions of internal Chinese rivals and the thunder of Mongol hooves.

JAPAN

For Japan, the Middle Ages saw the samurai enter the stage. *Samurai* is a 10th-century term, and initially applied to warriors who provided guard duty in the imperial capital, Kyoto. With time and change, however, the samurai came to be the elite of Japanese martial society, high-status fighters who served powerful nobles, this position confirmed not only by military skills but also, eventually, by inheritance.

The samurai stepped into the light during a turbulent time in Japanese political and social history. The imperial line of Japan had been established in the 7th century by the Yamato rulers, but Japan remained a country of rival clans and political manoeuvring. Two clans in particular – the Taira and Minamoto – came to blows in the 12th century over the imperial succession and influence at court. The Taira were victorious in the Heiji Rebellion of 1159–60, but in the subsequent Gempei War (1180–85), the Minamoto triumphed. Their leader, Minamoto no Yoritomo, in 1192 established himself in the new hereditary position of *shogun*, essentially a military dictatorship whose de facto power eclipsed that of the emperor. This position would remain until the 19th century, and the struggles to control or rebel against the shogunate would define much of Japanese samurai history, as would the perennial tensions between Japan's factious clans.

During the 13th century, however, the most pressing threat was external, in the form of the marauding Mongols. Kublai Khan would attempt two invasions of the Japanese mainland, in 1274 and 1281. The first was more of a reconnaissance-in-force than intended occupation, and it brought into contact two entirely distinct ways of making war. The samurai style of combat was influenced by broader ethical and aesthetic codes of behaviour, known as *kyuba no michi* (the way of horse and bow), but later referred to as *bushido* (the way of the warrior), although the latter is more of a 19th-century invention. The samurai warrior was meant to live a life of self-restraint, austerity, simplicity and humility, albeit balanced with high levels of martial skill and controlled ferocity on the battlefield.

Samurai warfare had a ritualistic aspect to it. Dressed in the elaborate but boxy *ō-yoroi* armour, the samurai of this period were

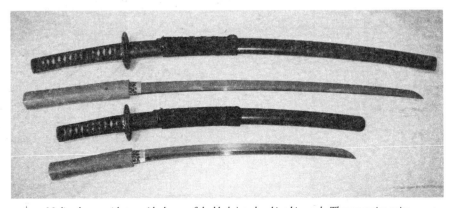

 Medieval samurai katana (the longer of the blades) and wakizashi swords. The samurai warrior would typically wear both of the blades in a matching pair, known as a daisho.

 Samurai ō-yoroi body armour was one of the most elaborate of armour types in history. Much of the armour was of lamellar construction, the plates tied together by strips of leather, deerskin or coloured silk.

principally mounted archers, fighting with the wood and bamboo *yumi* (bow), but also with the *yari* (spear) and the *naginata*, a long-bladed polearm. They also, famously, were exponents of some of the finest swords produced in history, worn in a pair (*daisho*) consisting of the long standard fighting sword, the *katana*, and the shorter back-up weapon, the *wakizashi*, both razor sharp and with long cutting edges. The *wakizashi*, or the shorter *tanto* dagger, were also used for that most defining of samurai practices, *seppuku*, or ritual suicide, which often involved driving the blade into one's own belly and making a strong longitudinal cut.

When samurai armies met on the battlefield, leading samurai would frequently dismount, exchanging arrows in an intense firefight before closing into close-quarters battle, where they demonstrated their abilities with spear, polearm and sword. There might also be a ritualistic element to the battle, samurai issuing challenges and seeking out suitable individuals to engage in single combat.

Although the samurai armies were certainly open to using subterfuge, misdirection, ambush and manoeuvre, much of their warfare was dictated by custom and accepted practice. Returning to the Mongol invasions, therefore, the Japanese troops who faced them at Hakata Bay were unsettled by the chaotic energy of the Mongol attack, with its archers, cavalry and early gunpowder bombs, and they were forced into a retreat before the Mongols about-turned and left. By 1281, therefore, the Japanese had judiciously fortified Hakata Bay, when they faced some 150,000 Mongol invaders, sailing in two great fleets. The defenders determinedly held off the first of the fleets, but then the elements stepped in on Japan's side: a thunderous typhoon wrecked the Mongols' ships, forcing the survivors to turn for home. This storm became known as the *kamikaze* (divine wind), a phrase that would come to have a very different resonance during the 20th century. The defeat of the Mongols brought some measure of peace to Japan, albeit not for long. In 1331, the Japanese Emperor, Go-Daigo, began a revolt against the Hojo shoguns, supported by the capable general Kusunoki Masashige. The consequent Wars of the Nanbokucho (Period of Southern and Northern Courts) resulted in two claims to the imperial throne, and also the death of Kusunoki at the epic Battle of Minatogawa on 5 July 1336; he committed *seppuku* when his resistance to the forces of the Ashikaga clan became futile. The Ashikaga rode the waves of victory and became the shoguns for the next two centuries, but the Onin War of 1467–77, essentially a civil war triggered by the shogunate succession, in turn led to the *Sengoku Jidai* (Period of Warring States), a series of endless inter-state and inter-clan conflicts that would last for more than a century. The samurai would be much in demand.

DIVIDED EUROPE AND THE REVOLUTION IN WARFARE

We complete our analysis of warfare in the Middle Ages by returning our focus to Western Europe, in particular the period between the 12th and the 15th centuries. The complexity of this period from an historical point of view is profound. Europe's existence under the umbrella of Christianity, ostensibly a religion of peace, forgiveness and restraint, did little to prevent the continent being engulfed in continual conflict, between states, between the Church and the state, between opposing branches of Christianity, between quarrelsome monarchs and nobles – there was scarcely a moment in which Europe could catch a breath of peace. It was also an era of profound change in terms of warfare, particularly led by England and France, but with key roles played by Spain, Italy, Switzerland and others.

The sheer number of European wars fought during this period precludes any detailed analysis of each, but we can point to two major engines driving conflict. The first was the clash of authority between the Catholic papacy, the French kings and the German Holy Roman Emperors, resulting in schisms that produced all manner of civil wars and international conflicts. For example, the Hohenstaufen Holy Roman Emperor Frederick I (r. 1155–90), aka Frederick 'Barbarossa' ('Red Beard' in Italian), undertook several campaigns into Italy between 1154 and 1174 in challenge to papal power and the authority of the Italian city-states, resisted from 1167 by the Lombard League. Frederick was a capable general, and had a particular knack in siege warfare. For instance, during the siege of Crema, which ran from July 1159 to February 1160, he progressively battered down the defences with catapults, rams and undermining; one of his siege towers was 32m (100ft) tall, with six storeys, and required 500 men to push it up to the battlements. Largely starved into surrender, Crema was eventually burned to the ground. But Frederick's ambitions in Italy were ultimately quashed at the Battle of Legnano on 29 May 1176, when Frederick's cavalry was broken against the determined resistance of a Milanese citizen army, Frederick having to flee the battlefield while most of his army was destroyed. Frederick went on to divert his attentions to the Crusades, and he drowned in a Turkish river in 1189.

The most enduring conflict of the later Middle Ages is what we refer to as the Hundred Years' War – actually a series of wars fought between England and France between 1337 and 1453 over English claims to the French throne. England itself had fought many internal wars by the time Edward III sailed with his invasion fleet on 22 June 1340, including the First Barons' War (1215–17) and Second Barons' War (1264–7), as well as major rebellions in Scotland and Wales. The Hundred Years' War initially saw England achieve victories that still resound in traditionally minded textbooks to this day – the naval Battle of Sluys (24 June 1340) and the land actions at Crécy (26 August

1346), Poitiers (19 September 1356) and, most famously, at Agincourt (25 October 1415), where some 6,000 fatigued English and Welsh foot soldiers under Henry V defeated 20,000–30,000 enemy troops, including the cream of France's knights. Yet these English victories were but landmarks on a long road to defeat, and eventually England lost all claims to the French throne. Compounding the defeat, the Hundred Years' War contributed towards the War of the Roses, a royal-succession civil war that blighted Britain between 1455 and 1487.

For much of the period between 1100 and 1500, it was the European knight who held the loftiest rank within the armies. Knights were an armoured cavalry elite, often identified with the nobility, although in fact many knights had 'risen from the ranks', serving long apprenticeships as pages and squires in knightly households until they were old enough to receive the honour of knighthood. On-the-spot battlefield knighthoods might also be conferred on individuals who had just shown bravery in action. Later in the period, however, knighthood did acquire a more hereditary aspect, as well as being infused with romantic literary notions of chivalry, presenting the knight as a form of holy warrior, noble in behaviour and ferocious in battle.

Knights were readily recognizable by their fine weaponry, equally fine armour – which by the end of the Middle Ages had taken the form of fully articulated plate armour – handsome horses and personal entourage. All this, of course, was extremely expensive; many individuals attempted, often unsuccessfully, to dodge knighthood and the costs that it would bring, which they had to bear personally. (Note that an armoured cavalryman might not necessarily have been a knight; these individuals were known as 'men-at-arms'.) By the 14th century, however, knights were increasingly paid from state coffers for their services, which provided a partial solution to the problems of recruitment.

The knight was typically a highly trained warrior, well versed in the theory and practice of warfare, and tested through either battlefield combat or the entertainingly brutal contests fought in martial tournaments. His primary tools of war were long double-edged swords, spiked war hammers, maces and wooden lances; he would fight both mounted and dismounted, the lance being the only weapon for purely mounted use.

The knight was not just a representation of a warrior elite, but was also emblematic of the divinely ordained hierarchy, the 'chain of being' that ran from the king or queen at the apex down to the lowest commoners at the bottom. A visible representation of this hierarchy was also the many mighty stone-built castles that proliferated around Europe, especially after the conquest of England by William the Conqueror in 1066.

Yet at the very end of the medieval period, a series of military changes began that would at first question, and then profoundly undermine, the confidence of this social order. Many of these changes would be fully played out in the period of the Renaissance, which we will examine in the next chapter. Here, therefore, we will briefly chart the major headline changes.

THE RISE OF THE INFANTRY

Up until the 14th century, cavalry had been the dominant component of armies for more than a millennium, but in the 1300s and 1400s infantry began their long return to authority. New weapons, particularly the European crossbow, the English longbow and early gunpowder firearms and artillery, meant that even plate armour was no longer sure protection against missile weaponry. Firearms and crossbows had a particular significance; they did not need the training from adolescence required to use a longbow properly, with the implication that a commoner with little warrior talent was now perfectly capable of killing a knight with generations of martial tradition and experience on his armoured shoulders. Furthermore, some nations began to innovate in more effective infantry formations. The Czech general Jan Žižka, leader of the Hussites, pioneered the use of armour-plated supply wagons and carts, forming them into a nearly impenetrable defensive *laager* when attacked, with infantry and artillery firing from the wagons and in the spaces between. The Swiss returned to the ancient principles of the tightly packed phalanx, equipping their troops with 6.4 m (21 ft) pikes and training them to move in a fast, aggressive mass that few opponents, for a time, could resist. In addition, kings increasingly took measures to develop proper standing armies, centrally funded from royal coffers, to free them from the limitations of feudal levies and the unpredictable behaviour of mercenaries. These new forces marked the true beginning of professional armies.

FORTIFICATIONS AND SIEGES

Sieges were regular events in medieval warfare, and would be for centuries to come. The challenge for besieging armies was that medieval fortifications grew ever stronger and more sophisticated during the Middle Ages. In the 10th century, the typical castle was of the motte-and-bailey type, consisting of a tall wooden or stone keep located on an elevated piece of ground (the motte), fronted or surrounded by an enclosed area of land, the bailey. By 1500, castles were far more impressive bastions, with two or more concentric curtain walls punctuated by towers at regular intervals, to ensure that no part of the wall was hidden from defensive fire; gateways were flanked by barbicans and towers, and were often accessible only via drawbridge. Water, moats and ditches provided outer defences, and many castles were located on inaccessible geographical features (especially in Britain), to cause further complications for a besieging army. Add the firepower of the defenders, which might include their own siege engines and, later, cannon artillery, and the medieval castle was a very stubborn obstacle.

Longbow

The English longbow was the pivotal instrument of victory at battles such as Crécy, Poitiers and Agincourt, and for a time the armies of Europe had nothing superior. The longbow was 167–200 cm (66–78 in) long, varying according to the height of the bowman, and was made from a single piece of wood, the most desirable being yew, with elm, oak, ash, hickory, hazel and maple as alternatives. Longbows had an exacting draw weight of up to 68 kg (150 lb), which took many years to master, bowmen began training in early youth. (Skeletons of medieval archers can often be identified by bone deformities, particularly relating to the vertebrae, shoulders and left arm.) But the result was a weapon that had an effective range of up to 320 m (350 yards), and which, when firing bodkin-head arrows, could pierce mail armour and, depending upon many variables, some plate armour. Fired in thousands, such arrows wreaked havoc upon enemy infantry and cavalry.

Stubborn, but not impregnable. Siege engines were largely the towers, rams, catapults, claws and other instruments of ancient times, but their power was now reaching its maximum expression. In the 12th century, the counterweight trebuchet appeared, which, in its mightiest varieties, was capable of hurling a 100 kg (220 lb) stone ball some 200 m (656 ft). In the 15th century, gunpowder cannon began to present a new threat to fortification walls, one that would eventually ensure the demise of the castle. At the siege of Constantinople in 1453, for example (see opposite),

Sultan Mehmet II's besieging army had several mighty bombards, the largest of which fired stone balls weighing more than 500 kg (1,100 lb). Such wall-cracking instruments meant that even the strongest of defences were no longer invulnerable.

GUNPOWDER

The advent of gunpowder weaponry was a tectonic shift in the history of warfare. Gunpower appears to have been invented around the 9th century in China, a country that utilized all manner of gunpowder weapons, including rockets and grenades. This combustible material reached Europe in the 13th century, and was at first applied to phenomenally crude vase-like artillery pieces, cast in iron or bronze and firing cumbersome arrows or stone balls. Steady improvements led to more conventional-looking iron 'bombards' firing iron or stone balls, mounted on fixed wooden frames or emplaced for firing on mounds of earth. These weapons, mostly muzzle-loading (although there were some breech-loading varieties), were both unpredictable and inaccurate, not least because of the poor quality of early gunpowder. The powder, and therefore the performance of cannon, was dramatically improved in the later 14th century by the process of 'corning', forming it into consistent grains, each grain containing the right volume of constituent elements. By the end of the Middle Ages, artillery was not only becoming the premier siege weapon, but when mounted on light wheeled carriages it also introduced the era of field artillery.

Small arms (infantry firearms) were a derivation of artillery, just scaled down for handheld use. The first firearms were basically nothing more than iron tubes drilled with a barrel and vent hole, sometimes strapped to a wooden haft for rudimentary control (the haft was held under the armpit). Loading and firing were acutely awkward manoeuvres, and the resulting shot was lucky to make a hit at under 30 m (33 yards). But improvements came. Gradually,

 The early medieval handgonnes were impressively awkward and inaccurate. Here the soldier grips the stock under his armpit while applying a smouldering slowmatch to the vent hole.

the barrels acquired fully fledged stocks, designed to be held in the shoulder, and the 'serpentine' mechanism gave mechanical efficiency to the act of applying a lit match to gunpower in the pan; now he had a trigger and a stock, the infantryman could devote more of his efforts to accurate aiming. These early muskets, known by various names (the French *arquebus* is one of the more common), began the age of standardized infantry firearms, although it would take at least a century before firearms offered genuine superiority over crossbows and bows.

On 29 May 1453, the great Byzantine capital of Constantinople fell to the Ottoman Turks of Sultan Mehmet II, after an exhaustingly violent siege action. It was truly the end of one of history's defining ages. Now gone were the last vestiges of Roman imperial structure that were laid down in the time of Augustus, and Islam, not Christianity, established a permanent foothold in the Balkans. In the following era, what we today call the Early Modern Period, the world saw some of the greatest cultural, scientific and artistic leaps since time began. Unfortunately for humanity, the same industrious invention would be applied to the practice of warfare.

CHAPTER 3
WAR IN THE EARLY
MODERN WORLD

The period between 1500 and 1750 was definitively formative in military history. In both the technology and the tactics of warfare, the era marks the boundary between the medieval and the modern, laying the foundation for military practices, theories and structures that exist to this day.

Few periods in the chronology of warfare match the 16th–mid-18th centuries for sheer historical complexity. This two-and-a-half century era, embracing what is classified in the West as the Renaissance, was an era in which faiths, empires and dynasties thundered in an almost unceasing drumroll of conflict, over causes that to modern eyes can appear almost unfathomable. Yet as so often occurs in sustained periods of conflict, war was the fuel for a restless innovation, concentrated in the hands of visionaries, commanders and inventors. And what innovations. Every aspect of warfare would experience a variety of revolutions, large and small – infantry tactics, the formation, size and structure of standing armies, infantry weapons, artillery, the roles and diversity of cavalry, fortifications and siegecraft, the shift to sail-powered warships, the international reach of warfare. Warfare was taking its next evolutionary step forwards.

A BATTLEFIELD TRANSFORMED

In the previous chapter, firearms and gunpowder artillery made their first appearance on the world's battlefields, unsettling centuries of social and martial hierarchy. In terms of artillery, the cannon of the early 16th century still had profound limitations – they were heavy and difficult to move (a standard heavy cannon could take as many as 23 horses to pull on its boxy carriage) and in the attempt to find the perfect balance between weight, mobility and firing range, the numbers of types and calibres multiplied excessively, making ammunition supply and manufacture problematic. From the middle part of the 16th century, however, forward-looking leaders such as Emperor Charles V and Henry II of France began to standardize artillery manufacture into a manageable number of specific types, ranging from lengthy culverins to deliver long-range fire on a relatively flat trajectory, down to stubby but thick-walled mortars for lobbing shells in high arcs over relatively short ranges (ideal for siege actions).

Building on this standardization, in the 17th century, artillery began to achieve the promise it had augured. Gustavus Adolphus, the King of Sweden from 1611–32, was, as we shall see, one of the most comprehensive military innovators of his age, transforming military practice in almost every regard. With artillery, Adolphus rationalized the types to three practical calibres – 24pdr, 12pdr and 3pdr (denoting the weight of roundshot) – thus optimizing artillery manufacture, while also improving the design of barrels and gunpowder to make the weapons lighter (and therefore more mobile) without diminishing power.

Experimentation continued through the 17th and 18th centuries to find the right spectrum of standardized calibres for battlefield use, while carriages were greatly improved, with two-wheeled types with light, spoked wheels and steady suspension making cannon far more transportable around the battlefield.

Infantry firearms also went through repeated improvements in design and functionality. During the second half of the 16th century, the musket was introduced. This initially matchlock weapon, heavier than the arquebus, delivered a longer range and greater penetration of armour, although reloading was slow and the long and weighty front end had to be supported on a forked rest during firing. Nevertheless, the musket gradually took over from the arquebus by the end of the century.

What was still needed, however, was a faster and more efficient firing mechanism, to increase loading times and therefore rates of fire. The wheellock mechanism was developed around 1500. It used a spring-loaded steel wheel that, when released by pulling the trigger, spun against a piece of pyrite, generating the sparks to cause pan ignition and firing. The great advantage of the wheellock was that it could be loaded and held ready for later use (you couldn't conceal a smouldering matchlock in your pocket). It was principally used in cavalry pistols, one-handed weapons that mounted troops could wield conveniently from horseback. However, they were

 An impressively ornate wheellock pistol made for Maximilian I of Bavaria (r. 1597–1623). Wheellocks were expensive instruments of war, and were largely found only in the hands of elite and affluent cavalry.

79

prohibitively expensive to manufacture for large armies, so they tended to be a weapon of the elite.

A British military Short Land Pattern Musket, one of several varieties of Land Pattern Musket known collectively as the 'Brown Bess'. It was one of the defining small arms of the 18th and 19th centuries, used across the British Empire and North America.

The great leap forwards came with the invention of the snaphaunce lock in the 1560s. This used a piece of flint, gripped in the jaws of a spring-loaded, trigger-activated hammer, to generate the ignition sparks when it dropped on to a steel piece above the pan. The snaphaunce led to the improved flintlock of the early 1600s, a firing mechanism that was relatively simple (hence ideal for mass manufacture of standardized weapons), reliable (at least by the standards of the day) and could be used by even the humblest infantryman. Firing rates improved to around four rounds per minute, aided over time by the introduction of cartridges that contained pre-measured gunpowder, ball and wad in one convenient unit (this was possibly another of Gustavus' inventions) and of the double-ended iron ramrod by the Prussians in *c.*1718, which was faster and more durable than the single-ended wooden ramrods used previously. Muskets were also lightened in weight to about 5 kg (11 lb), removing the need for the front rest and making them properly portable infantry weapons.

Another advancement in firearms design was the bayonet. By fitting a bayonet to his weapon, the infantryman could change his role in an instant to that of a pikeman. The first bayonets were plug bayonets, which literally fitted into the muzzle of the weapon, preventing the weapon from being fired when the bayonet was in use. In *c.*1680, however, the socket bayonet was invented, the blade offset on the side of a cylindrical and open-ended metal socket that fitted *around* the muzzle, meaning that even with the bayonet fitted, the weapon could still be loaded and fired.

It was the invention of the socket bayonet, in addition to the rise of artillery, that would eventually see the pikemen disappear from the field of battle. Yet edged and penetrating weapons such as swords, lances, halberds and pikes would continue to play a crucial role in warfare for much of the period of this chapter, not least because battle still went to close quarters.

Siegecraft and Fortifications

The invention of artillery changed fortification and siegecraft permanently. From the 16th century, fortifications that were elevated in height and built on lofty ground – basically the castles of the medieval era – were suddenly little more than accessible and easily hit targets for gunners. (A further consideration is that cannon perform at their best when the barrel is slightly elevated on a high target, because of the improved compression of the gunpowder and shot under gravity.) In the 16th and 17th centuries, therefore, military engineers and architects such as Baldassare Peruzzi, Vincenzo Scamozzi, Sébastien Le Prestre de Vauban and Menno van Coehoorn turned their thinking to new generations of fortification, better able both to withstand a cannon-armed besieging army and also with increased defensive capabilities. Fortifications therefore became lower and heavier, the outer walls protected by earthen slopes to soak up cannonballs; projecting triangular bastions on which artillery was mounted to give all-round defensive fire; and broad ditches to break up cavalry attacks, the outer side of which was further protected by a sloping terrace or glacis, itself defended by cannon.

For the besieging armies, these structures completely rewrote the rules of siegecraft, especially as many classic methods of bringing down walls – such as mining – were now far harder to apply. Siegecraft therefore became a matter of sapping: digging covered trenches forwards towards the enemy fortification, under the cover of long-range guns, and establishing successive artillery positions closer and closer to the outer walls and defences. Once the artillery and infantry musketeers were close enough to deliver sufficient suppressive fire and destruction, then a mass infantry attack could be launched to overwhelm the defences.

 This aerial view of the Ciudadala de Jaca in northern Spain illustrates the geometric principles of defence that influenced fortress design during the Early Modern period.

This quick summary does not do full justice to the intricate science and tactical thought that went into Renaissance siegecraft and fortification, the requirements of which were another reason, like that of the artillery arm and military engineering, that armies increasingly needed permanent technically skilled professionals in their ranks.

ARMIES AND TACTICS

During the 16th century, many wars were fought with relatively small standing armies, supplemented by sizeable contingents of mercenaries. During the 17th century, however, the composition, organization and administration of armies changed significantly, pushed on by Gustavus and other key individuals such as Louis XIV and John of Nassau. Change was actually essential. Armies in this era were becoming ever larger, which in turn meant that maintaining them and deploying them on campaign was a massive drain on the state economy. (During some major wars, up to 90 per cent of a national budget could be allocated to military expenditure.) There was also a shift away from relying on mercenaries, with professional standing armies, funded by the state, becoming the norm.

During the Renaissance, armies became steadily organized according to standardized units, including some of the unit types we know today – companies, battalions and regiments. These units were permanent parts of the standing army, not temporary entities developed for a campaign, and were kept at strength with a regular influx of recruits. The system dramatically improved the chain of command, training, logistics and the sense of unit identity, with individual units establishing a sense of combat lineage and tradition. The armies were also professionalizing, not least because weapons such as artillery demanded higher levels of technical skill.

Gustavus, for example, replaced civilian contractor artillerymen with professional soldiers, to ensure that essential knowledge was contained within the ranks and passed on effectively to future generations. Significantly, the non-familiar military system of ranks also took shape in this period, establishing a clear sense of seniority and progression within the armies.

Tactically, there were also major changes. At the beginning of the era, the optimal infantry combat formation was the 'Spanish square', so called because it was codified by King Ferdinand of Spain in 1505. The Spanish gathered their infantry into a mass of about 1,000 men known as a *colunela* (column), the column containing all the essential infantry fighting elements – arquebusiers, pikemen and halberdiers. In action, three *colunelas* were typically formed into a larger formation known as a *tercio*, and it was this that was the 'Spanish square'. The Spanish-type formation typically placed the pikemen (the larger percentage of the formation) at the centre, with the arquebusiers set out on the flanks in support.

During the late 16th and 17th centuries, three major changes occurred in the way infantry was handled. First, the numbers of arquebusiers/musketeers increased in proportion to other arms, until they became the majority. Second, innovators such as Maurice of Nassau improved the rates of volley fire by rotating the front ranks of shooters with ones behind; subsequent improvements would see musketeers adopting simultaneous kneeling/standing ranks to increase the volume of fire. Third, infantry formations became more linear and thinner, often just four to six ranks in depth. This innovation resulted in major increases in the frontage of infantry delivering fire. Combined with the roaring power of artillery, gunpowder attrition was now the central pillar of land warfare.

The 16th–18th centuries were also a time of change for European cavalry. The rise of firearms and artillery meant that the heavily armoured knights of the medieval age were truly confined to the past. During the Renaissance, the types of cavalry diversified, partly through the Europeans' encounters with the light, fast-moving cavalry of the Islamic traditions. Heavy cavalry remained important for mass of attack; the principal form of heavy cavalry during this age were the cuirassiers, mounted on the largest steeds and wearing a heavy metal cuirass breastplate. But beneath the cuirassiers and similar types, intermediate and light cavalry proliferated, including hussars, dragoons and lancers, each with their own role and identity. This spectrum of cavalry was applied flexibly and dynamically; in addition to making battlefield charges, they were used for screening, reconnaissance, pursuit, and other duties. The era also gave birth to the horse artillery arm, in which all gun crews were mounted, meaning that they could keep pace with cavalry manoeuvres and deploy guns quickly and frequently to exploit tactical opportunities.

Pistol firearms and carbines (shortened versions of full-length muskets) expanded the cavalry arsenal and brought some fresh tactics. In the *caracole*, a body of cavalry would ride up to the enemy infantry ranks, turn flush to its front, draw and discharge their pistols (three were usually carried), and then ride back to reload while the next unit of cavalry moved up to perform the same action. The effectiveness of the *caracole* is very much open to debate – it was vulnerable to both infantry counterfire (which was much heavier than anything the cavalry could deliver) and to cavalry countercharge – and it had declined in use by the end of the 17th century.

NAVAL WARFARE

The greatest of the revolutions in warfare during the Renaissance are to be found in the field of naval warfare. At the beginning of the period, the oar-powered galley was still the primary warship, designed for ramming and boarding actions and lightly armed on the bows with small-calibre cannon. Sailing warships were primarily used for logistics or as troop platforms. But during the 16th century, and especially under the intensive shipbuilding programmes of England's Henry VIII (r. 1509–47), new generations of fighting sail, in the form of carracks and galleons, emerged. In the British expression, these had lower 'castles' – the raised platforms at the front and back of the main deck – and a focus on maximizing onboard artillery; the rest of the world soon followed these principles. The invention of the gunport was crucial. This hinged door, set in the hull of the ship, allowed cannon to be mounted in the lower decks, their barrels projecting out through the open gunports when in action. The configuration had crucial implications: it meant that a ship could carry many tons of cannon firepower without making the vessel top-heavy and unstable. It also meant that warships could now deliver a fearsome 'broadside', engaging the enemy ships with a rippling barrage that was greater than that some land armies could muster.

The Royal Navy also came to develop the rating system for warships, classifying them according to size of the ship and the corresponding number of guns. There were six rates, with the first, second and third rates being classed as 'ships of the line', meaning that they could take their place in the primary line of battle. A first-rate warship had more than 80 guns arranged across three decks; by the end of the 18th century, it typically had more than 100 heavy cannon and 850 crew. Sixth-rate vessels, by contrast, were small frigates or 'post-ships', supporting about 20–28 guns.

The age of fighting sail resulted in wholesale shifts in ship design, tactics and naval strategy. The four key players in warship building in Europe were Britain, Spain, France and the Netherlands, but it was Britain in particular that honed the cutting edge of naval development. Within the Royal Navy, there was a focus on

The English carrack Henry Grace à Dieu was one of the world's greatest warships when it was commissioned in 1514. It had a complement of more than 700 men and was armed with 184 guns of various calibres.

excellence and speed in gunnery, assisted by technical developments in rope-controlled recoil that dramatically speeded up reloading times. Tactically, the British naval commanders sought to bring their warships into close range and smash the enemy vessels into submission or sinking. The French, by contrast, often sought to conserve its fleet (especially in the later part of our period), generally preferring to bring down the enemy's mainmasts to disable their ships then, if the tide of the battle was swinging against them, escape rather than engage in blunt exchanges of fire to the point of destruction. (There were, of course, many exceptions to these principles in the fluid reality of an engagement and according to a commander's preferences.)

The development of fighting sail now made the world's seas and oceans genuine battlegrounds. More importantly, they internationalized conflicts in a way not seen previously. Thus what was essentially a European war could now be fought in parallel thousands of miles away in the Caribbean Sea, Atlantic Ocean, Indian Ocean and the Pacific. War's reach was now far greater.

ISLAMIC WARS

In the previous chapter, we witnessed a seminal moment in world history – the fall of Constantinople to Sultan Mehmed II of the Ottoman Empire, the apogee of expansionist Islam. Islam remained a potent force throughout the 16th and 17th centuries, concentrated principally in three main empires: that of the Ottoman Turks, Safavid Persians and the Mogul Indians.

The rise of the Ottomans was particularly notable. They, embracing some aspects of modernization, especially in artillery, had a formidable army, and used it to carve out a huge empire which, at its height under Mehmed IV (r. 1648–87), covered much of North Africa, almost all of the Balkans and south-eastern Europe, Syria, Palestine, Iraq and the eastern Arabian Peninsula. Its expansion inevitably brought it into frequent conflict with others, especially the Europeans and the Safavid Persians, the resulting battles offering the Ottomans opportunities to demonstrate the superiority of their Janissary infantry and impressive cavalry. Landmark engagements along the way include Chaldiran (23 August 1514), when the Ottomans decisively defeated the Safavids in north-western Iran; Raydaniya (22 January 1517) in Egypt, which led to the subsequent capture of Cairo and the collapse of the Mamluk sultanate; and Mohács (29 August 1526), when Suleiman I the Magnificent (r. 1520–66) defeated King Louis of Hungary on the approaches to the Hungarian capital, Buda. From this victory, Hungary became an Ottoman vassal state, and three years later Suleiman attempted to capture Vienna by siege, although failed in this attempt.

With every empire in history, there is typically a defining moment, or at least period, in history from which we can map that empire's decline. Although the Ottoman Empire would survive in some form or another until the 20th century, we can point to the great naval battle of Lepanto on 7 October 1571 as a true turning point. This epic clash of galleys off the coast of Greece brought the Ottoman fleet into battle with the combined fleets of the Holy League, a collection of European forces organized by Pope Pius V, and including forces of the Habsburg Empire. (The Habsburg Empire was an extensive swathe of European territory ruled over by the Habsburg Monarchy, centred mainly in Austria, the ruler of the House of Habsburg also being the Holy Roman Emperor for the period 1440–1740.) In a clattering, violent clash of oars, bows and weapons, the Ottoman fleet was utterly crippled. Although the Ottomans quickly rebuilt their fleet the following year, Ottoman naval power was curtailed internationally, especially when set against the backdrop of the steady then meteoric rise in European naval power during this chapter's period. Ottoman power in the

Türkisches Militär (Janitscharen).

 Uniforms of the Ottoman Empire's elite Janissary infantry. The Janissaries were originally slave soldiers, but their loyalty to the empire and their discipline in battle were infamous.

Mediterranean began to contract, cemented by failed attempts to capture Malta in 1565 and Vienna in 1683. A truly crushing battlefield defeat at Zenta (in modern Serbia) by Austrian forces, led by Prince Eugéne Francis of Savoy–Carignano – one among the great military commanders of the Renaissance – wrecked the Ottoman army, and Prince Eugéne hammered further nails into the Ottoman coffin at the Battle of Petrovaradin in 1716 and the Siege of Belgrade in 1717.

Beyond the Ottoman Empire and the territories of the Middle East, Islamic empires and states were established or expanded by force widely across Africa, Central Asia and the Indian subcontinent. In North Africa, Islam pushed southwards from the 10th century, such that by 1500 it had extended deep into sub-Saharan Africa. In North-west Africa, Ottoman-backed Morocco was one of the most powerful states, its modern multi-ethnic army more than capable of taking on European intrusions into the region. At the Battle of Al Kasr al Kebir in Morocco on 4 August 1578, for example, the Moroccan army of Abd al-Malik destroyed a Portuguese army under the young King Sebastian of Portugal (r. 1557–78), although both monarchs were killed in the fighting. Further south, African armies also fought one another on a regular basis. Sometimes this was on account of clashes between religions and sometimes for basic territorial ambition, but from the 14th century onwards a major conflict-driver was the slave trade. The more powerful African states and empires, such as the Mali, Songhai, Asante, Dahomey and Oyo, conducted large-scale military expeditions against weaker neighbours, acquiring tens of thousands of slaves for trading to the Islamic states around the Mediterranean or, later, to European slave traders.

Further east still, the 16th–18th centuries saw India experience the impact of Islamic invasions from Central Asia, although Islam itself had been establishing itself in India since the 7th century. In

1525, the Uzbek warrior king Zahiruddin Muhammad – better known as 'Babur' (Tiger) – invaded northern India at the head of 12,000 men, and on 21 April 1526 fought a far larger army of Sultan Ibrahim Lodi at Panipat, about 90 km (55 miles) north of Delhi. Babur, deploying massed cannon and matchlocks, defeated his opponents, despite Ibrahim bringing 1,000 war elephants to the fight, and in so doing established the beginnings of the Mughal Empire in South Asia.

The expansion of this empire was driven particularly by Babur's grandson, Akbar, who won another great victory at Panipat in November 1556, by which time most of northern and central India was under Mughal rule. An alliance of Muslim states opened the door to Islamic penetration of southern India when it defeated the Kingdom of Vijayanagar in battle at Talikota on 23 January 1565, although they subsequently came under Mughal domination through the expansions of Muhi-ud-Din Muhammad, aka Aurangzeb, who ruled over the Mughal Empire from 1658 to 1707 and took it to its greatest extent, governing 158 million subjects. During his reign, however, the empire also began the decline that would accelerate in the 18th century. The Mughals found themselves unable to counter a growing Hindu Maratha Confederacy, who would eventually take Delhi itself in 1771.

JAPAN, CHINA AND EAST ASIA

From 1468 to 1615, Japan went through what is known as the Sengoku Period (Age of Warring States). The title is apt: for nearly 150 years, the country was enmired in near-constant conflict, as rival *daimyo* (feudal lords) struggled for supremacy.

From the general melee of power struggles, certain individuals naturally rose to the top – men who are today legends of Japanese military and social history. Oda Nobunaga (1534–82) is regarded as one of the earliest of Japan's unifiers, who between 1560 and his

A violent scene from the First Battle of Panipat in India on 21 April 1526 shows the death of Sultan Ibrahim Lodi, beheaded as he tried to retreat from Mughal forces.

death in 1582 managed to take over most of Honshu island. A man absorbed by martial affairs from boyhood, Nobunaga later showed confidence, competence and innovation in leading armies on campaign and into battle. He quickly racked up a series of startling victories. At Okehazama in June 1560, for example, Nobunaga defeated *c.*25,000 soldiers of Imagawa Yoshimoto with just 3,000 of his own warriors, through a mixture of deception, ambush and clever use of terrain. The greatest of his victories, however, was at Nagashino on 28 June 1575. This time, Nobunaga had no shortage of men – his forces numbered 38,000 – and he innovatively used 3,000 arquebusiers, positioned behind a wooden palisade, to shatter the initial samurai cavalry charge of Takeda Katsuyori, completing the victory through a hard-fought close-quarters fight with sword and spear.

Nobunaga died in 1582 by his own hand – he committed suicide during the last stages of the coup led by his samurai general Akechi Mitsuhide. Into Nobunaga's shoes, however, stepped Toyotomi Hideyoshi, a *daimyo*, another of Nobunaga's generals and a man of such military talent that he is sometimes referred to as the 'Napoleon of Japan'. On 2 July 1582, he secured his revenge over Mitsuhide by defeating his army at Yamazaki (Mitsuhide fled the battle and was later murdered), and he then went on to crush the forces of Shibata Katsuie at Shizugatake (21 April 1583) and the Hōjō clan in the Kanto region at the siege of Odawara in 1590.

Hideyoshi died in 1598, but the equally formidable warlord Tokugawa Ieyasu (1542–1616) completed the process of fully reunifying Japan. Although Ieyasu had in the past been an opponent of both Nobunaga and Hideyoshi, he eventually became one of their most competent allies. On 21 October 1600, he took a landmark victory in Japanese history at Sekigahara, crushing an alliance led by Ishida Mitsunari. This cleared the way, in 1603, for

Ieyasu to take the position of shogun, and the Tokugawa dynasty would rule Japan in relative peace for the next 250 years.

Japan's military efforts during the Sengoku Period were not just directed internally. In the early 1590s, Toyotomi Hideyoshi became more international in outlook, and planned an invasion of Korea. His intention was to invade and occupy the Korean Peninsula and advance north to campaign in China. The invasion was launched on 23 May 1592, the first Japanese troops landing at Busan, and over the next few days Japan put ashore more than 200,000 soldiers. The initial campaign seemed promising for the invaders, as they defeated opposition forces in several major battles and sieges. Then the problems set in. As the Japanese pushed on into the Korean interior, they became prey to a biting Korean guerrilla warfare, which inflicted attrition and strained logistics. More important, at sea the Korean navy – which included several of the groundbreaking ironclad 'turtle ships', warships literally covered with metal plate armour – commanded by the talented Admiral Yi Sunshin, preyed on Japanese naval logistics. Yi would defeat the Japanese in open battle on several occasions in 1592, such as at Hansando and Danghangpo, and in 1597 at Myongyang. The latter was the occasion of the second Japanese invasion of Korean; the first invasion had effectively collapsed in 1594, with most of the Japanese forces withdrawn. In the second invasion, again the Japanese won early battles, but building pressures at sea and on land – especially with the arrival of sizeable Chinese formations committed by the Ming Emperor – pushed the Japanese back. The second invasion burned itself out in 1598, its failure aided by the death of Hideyoshi.

Just as peace and order were beginning to establish themselves in Japan, China entered a time of convulsions. At the turn of the 17th century, China was ruled by a weakening Ming dynasty, whose greatest threat came from Nurhaci, a rebellious chieftain of the

 Several illustrious women also appear in the ranks of samurai history. Here we see, on horseback, the great Tomoe Gozen, a 12th-century samurai known for her beauty, bravery and sill with a bow and sword.

Jianzhou Juchen, a Manchurian tribe that rebelled against Ming rule in about 1610. Nurhaci's power swelled as the Ming's declined, aided by his effective military–administrative organization of Juchen, Mongol and Chinese forces into 'banners' (see feature box). Collectively known as the Manchu, the forces of Nurhaci and his successors made two failed attempts to invade China in the 1620s, both pushed back by the Ming general Yuan Chonghuan. But in 1636–7, the Manchu successfully took Korea, then in 1644 Beijing fell, ushering in the age of the Qing dynasty.

Victory did not bring peace. The Manchu found themselves trying to control and consolidate a territory of breathtaking extent, riven with political compromises and local power bases, and so wars against enemies foreign and domestic rumbled on for much of the 17th century.

One notable military action, which demonstrated the capability of the Manchu way of war, came in 1696, when the Qing Emperor Kangxi personally led a momentous army of 80,000 men across the Gobi desert to fight the Dzungar Khanate of Mongolia, part of what is known as the First Dzungar–Qing War (1687–97). The journey took an epic 80 days, but Kangxi's attention to logistics – he had assembled 1,333 supply carts to support the expedition – meant his army arrived capable of fighting. At the Battle of Jao Modo, fought in June 1696, the Manchu army utterly destroyed the Dzungar forces who, without gunpowder weaponry, were unable to find a response to Qing artillery and muskets.

The Bannermen

The Banner system, first organized by Nurhaci, was a key ingredient of the Manchu victory over the Chinese in the first half of the 17th century, and of its subsequent military campaigns and governance. In its first incarnation in 1601, all Manchu warriors were organized into four companies, each of 300 men and each distinguished by its own coloured banner – red, white, blue and yellow. As the Manchu army grew in scale, four more banners were added in 1615, using the same colours but bordered in red, except for the red banner, which was bordered in white. In 1635, the Mongol tribes allied to the Manchu were arranged into eight of their own banners, and in 1642 another eight banners of Chinese were added.

These 24 banners, each now consisting of thousands of warriors, were not just a way of rationalizing the army. They also served as a framework for civil administration, including taxation and conscription. Following the establishment of the Qing dynasty, the 24 banners remained in place, most of the forces concentrated in Beijing, but with others based around the country in security roles. The Qing also founded an 'Army of the Green Standard', a widespread force of non-Manchu units, used to police the vast country.

THE AMERICAS

Before the 16th century, the Americas had been ruled by tribal societies, either nomadic or settled, often with strong albeit ritualistic warrior codes. In both North and South America, war between these tribes was frequent but tended to be limited in scope, often focused more on raiding and prisoner-taking rather than the wholesale destruction of the enemy, although at times the wars could be extremely bloody. Most young men, at least those not of a slave class, would have to prove themselves capable hunters and fighters to come of age, and brave and fearless spirit in war was essential to gaining his respect in the tribe or people. The typical weapons were bows and arrows, javelins, spears, clubs, axes and daggers, the impact weapons typically made from wood and various types of stone (metal weaponry was rare in the Americas before the arrival of the Europeans), with some ingenuity. The Aztec *maquahuitl* club, for instance, consisted of a heavy hardwood paddle club edged with 'blades' of flint or obsidian. In addition to the use of basic (although often highly ornamented) shields, some tribes also wore early forms of body armour, made from materials such as padded hide, quilted fabrics, and pieces of wood and horn.

The military experience of the American tribes changed profoundly and, for them, disastrously, with the arrival of European invaders and settlers in the 15th–17th centuries. Pre-Columbian South America (i.e. South America before the expedition of Christopher Columbus in 1492) was dominated by several extensive, highly sophisticated warrior empires, including the Aztecs, with its powerbase in present-day Mexico; the Incas, who ruled over Peru, most of Chile and many other parts of eastern South America; and the Mayan peoples of Mexico and Central America. Although they were undoubtedly formidable empires, Spanish colonialism in the 16th century brought them up against foes and weaponry the likes of which they could not have imagined.

The beginning of the fall of the Aztec Empire began in November 1518, when the conquistador Hernán Cortés landed with an army of 600 men, 17 horses and ten cannon on the Yucatán Peninsula in south-eastern Mexico. Cortés augmented his small force by allying himself with the anti-Aztec Tlaxcala people. Intimidated by the confidence and strangeness of the Spanish (the Aztecs had never seen horses or gunpowder weapons, for example), the Aztec emperor Montezuma II at first allowed the Spanish to enter the capital, Tenochtitlán. However, as their abuses of power became clear, the Aztecs rebelled, with hundreds of Spaniards being killed in Tenochtitlán during the 'Night of Sorrows' (30 June– 1 July 1520).

Cortés – who had been away from the city at the time – now with about 370 soldiers plus his Tlaxcalan allies, nevertheless inflicted a heavy defeat upon the Aztecs at Otumba on 7 July 1520, a final charge by his cavalry with sword and lance breaking the Aztec army. Then, the following year, between 31 May and 14 August 1521, he laid siege to Tenochtitlán, this time with an army augmented by other anti-Aztec tribes. The siege set a wearying rhythm of attack and counter-attack, the Spanish forces driving into the city across causeways during the day, killing everyone they met, and retreating out of the city before nightfall. Finally, Aztec resistance collapsed in August 1521, much of the population dying either from starvation, smallpox (a European import that devastated the Native American population) and the subsequent massacre.

The leading figure in the conquest of the Incas was the conquistador Francisco Pizarro. In 1532, Pizarro, with a force of Spanish soldiers numbering only about 150–200 men, nevertheless marched on Cajamarca, the city where the Inca emperor Atahualpa was based. This was an act of considerable bravado, given that the Incas had at this time an army of about 40,000 men, although a recent civil war and a smallpox epidemic had severely weakened the empire. The encounter between Atahualpa and Pizarro began with formal cordiality, but on 16 November 1532 the Spanish troops ambushed the Inca royal party, taking Atahualpa prisoner and killing most of his entourage. This act cut the heart out of the Incas in an instant, and the Spanish subsequently captured the Inca capital, Cuzco, without a fight and later quashed any attempts at rebellion.

European colonization of North America began in the late 16th century, with Spanish landings in Florida and then British landings in Virginia. Settlements proliferated and grew, with the Dutch and the French also establishing themselves on the continent. During the 17th century, the incipient colonization of North America

 The Inca emperor Atahualpa is surrounded and captured by Spanish forces at the Battle of Cajamarca in 1532. The Spanish superiority in firepower and mobility is evident in this artwork.

naturally brought the settlers into conflict with the Native American tribes who inhabited the lands, especially in the woodlands of the north-east. On 22 March 1622, for example, warriors of the Powhatan Confederacy swept down upon the English settlement at the mouth of the James River in Virginia, slaughtering many of the settlers. Atrocity tended to breed counter-atrocity during this age. When, in July 1636, a European trader was murdered by Pequot warriors in Connecticut, a counter-raid by the settler militia – supported by allied Native American tribes – massacred the occupants of the Pequot village of Mystic, an action from which the Pequots never recovered as a tribe.

The destruction of Mystic speaks of the fact that the wars in North America in the 17th and 18th century were never simply a matter of settlers vs Native Americans, but also saw the settlers allied with Native American tribes in campaigns against common enemies. The so-called Iroquois Wars, for example, pitted five nations of the Iroquois Confederacy against their Huron rivals in nearly 60 years of off-and-on fighting (1640–98), the Iroquois also facing French army forces. Both sides adapted their fighting based on encounters with their enemies. The French, for example, learned the skills of small-group raiding and ambush, while many Native American tribes became enthusiastic adopters of firearms and also mastered the skills of horsemanship, fighting from horseback with bow, spear and club.

WAR IN EUROPE

The wars in Europe between 1500 and 1750 defy easy compression into a historical narrative. Speaking in the very broadest terms, the conflicts were generated along four major fault lines running through European politics and culture: the clash between the Protestant and Catholic faiths following the Protestant Reformation in the 16th century; dynastic disputes, particularly regarding the succession of monarchs; territorial rivalries and expansionism; and early battles of colonizing empires, sometimes fought hundreds or even thousands of miles from the European landmass. In reality, the many European wars of this period were frequently a mix of several or all of these influences, clashes between individual states often triggering outside alliances and interests that brought continent-wide conflict. The intensity and frequency of fighting in Europe created a ghastly laboratory of warfare, in which technology and tactics made seminal leaps, often under the direction of some of the greatest commanders in military history.

The wars of Renaissance Europe were often of impressive duration. Fought between 1494 and 1559, for example, the Italian Wars were triggered when Charles VIII of France (r. 1483–98) invaded Italy to pursue a dynastic claim. This triggered an escalation that saw France pitted against a 'Holy League' of forces formed by Pope Julius II in 1511, principally those of Italy and Spain. The war was especially significant for the battlefield innovations of the Spanish commander Gonzalo Fernández de Córdoba, who combined pikemen and arquebusiers in the potent new formation that came to be copied throughout Europe. In this protracted war, both sides experienced their share of victories and defeats. Some of the landmark battles include Cerignola (28 April 1503), where Córdoba smashed a French attack (supported by Swiss pikemen mercenaries) with his pikemen and arquebusiers, and Ravenna (11 April 1512), a French victory over the Spanish that involved a two-hour artillery duel between the opposing cannon. As so often occurred with these conflicts, the war ended not so much with a decisive victory on one side, but rather a series of compromises and treaties, agreed by nations exhausted of war.

The Protestant Reformation, initiated by the German theologian Martin Luther in 1517, began with a challenge to religious practices. Yet as Europe progressively divided itself into Protestant or Catholic branches of Christianity, this religious divide fuelled a fresh generation of conflicts. The wars were, of course, more complex than just matters of faith – the Christian alignment of states, empires and monarchs had profound political implications as well – but the spiritual dimension of these conflicts allowed all manner of atrocities and inhumanity to thrive in the name of the 'true' faith.

The pattern of the religious wars of the 16th and 17th centuries was complex. In the 1560s, France collapsed into a Catholic vs Protestant civil war, the latter represented by the Calvinistic Huguenots and the former by the royal house. Typical of the age, the local war had an international flavour to it. Both sides used foreign mercenaries – the Protestants, for example, employed many German *Landsknechte* (see feature box) and German heavy cavalry known as *Reiters* ('riders'), while Swiss pikemen bulked out the ranks of the Catholics. (There was much rivalry between these mercenary forces, and little mercy if one took the other prisoner.) There was also a lot of foreign state intervention, with England, Scotland and Navarre backing the Protestants and Spain and Savoy supporting the Catholics.

Landsknechte Mercenaries

The *Landsknechte* were German mercenary infantry who found themselves in heavy demand during the late 15th–early 17th centuries. They were first raised in 1486 by the Holy Roman Emperor Maximilian I, and their ranks grew significantly upon a battlefield reputation of ferocity and professionalism. The Landsknechte were mainly pikemen, although they also fought with halberds, a fearsome two-hand sword called *Zweihänder* (double-hander), arquebuses and a standard-issue short sword

---

 The pike was a decisive weapon in European history for more than a century. Here the artist Hans Holbein shows the claustrophobic horror of a mass pike battle.

called a *Katzbalger*. On the battlefield, they tended to fight in a deep square formation, with *Doppelsöldner* (double-pay men) in the front ranks, so called because by opting to fight at the front, a far riskier position, they received double pay. The *Landsknechte* were a crucial component of the Holy Roman imperial army for more than a century, but the changing technologies and tactics of warfare put them into decline by the early 17th century.

The first major battle of the war was at Dreux on 19 December 1562, but many more were fought until Protestant Henry of Navarre, by this time crowned Henry IV of France, defeated a Holy League army at Coutras (1587), Arques (1589), Ivry (1590) and Amiens (1597). The Edict of Nantes in 1598 brought the French Wars of Religion to an uneasy close (the 17th century saw further religious conflict in France), by which time as many as 3 million people might have died from violence and the associated disease and famine.

France was not the only arena of battle for the European religious wars. A similar lengthy conflict was fought in the Netherlands, following the Dutch Protestant revolt against Spanish Habsburg rule in the 1560s. England also came to blows with Catholic Spain, a clash most famously represented when Spain's Philip II attempted an invasion of England with his 'Spanish Armada' in 1588. In a battle that came to define England's rising naval supremacy, an English fleet under Lord Howard of Effingham and Sir Francis Drake intercepted and engaged the 130-strong Spanish fleet with their superior gunnery in late July, eventually driving the Spanish survivors into the North Sea, from where they endeavoured to return to Spain by sailing around Scotland and Ireland, rather than try to pass through the Channel again. Adverse weather and onboard disease took a further toll on the Spanish shipping; some 63 ships were lost in total, and England remained safe from invasion.

Although the religious wars in Europe certainly consumed millions of lives, they were not the most destructive conflict of this belligerent era. That honour goes to the Thirty Years' War, an almost global conflict fought from 1618 to 1648 for a bewildering variety of religious, dynastic and territorial reasons, triggered by the Habsburg Empire's efforts to quash Protestantism in Bohemia. The fighting sucked most European nations into a war that would cost an estimated 8 million lives.

The Thirty Years' War was a proving ground for many of the new tactics and technologies of the age, conducted in battles of epic scale – the Battle of First Breitenfeld (17 September 1631), for example, saw a Swedish/Saxony army of 42,000 face an imperial army of 35,000. Breitenfeld was close fought, but ultimately a landmark victory for Gustavus Adolphus. Indeed, it was the Thirty Years' War that cemented Gustavus' reputation as one of the finest military minds of the century, although his death at the Battle of Lützen (16 November 1632) – his final victory – was a potent blow to the Protestant cause. His passing doubtless contributed to the destruction of a Swedish army at Nördlingen in September 1634, although the rise of another highly capable Swedish commander – Lennart Torstensson – saw an imperial army dominated at the Battle of Second Breitenfeld on 12 November 1642. (An indicator of Torstensson's formidable personality was that although he was crippled by arthritis, he insisted on being carried around the battlefield on a litter to give his commands.)

The Thirty Years' War ended with the Peace of Westphalia in 1648, with the Habsburgs humbled and Sweden and France rising powers in Europe. But even as this great war subsided, others were either raging or flaring up.

From 1642, England was caught in the grinding mill of its seminal civil war, fought between the Royalists loyal to Charles I (r. 1625–49) and Parliamentarians, led by Oliver Cromwell. In the first year of fighting, the Royalists largely had the upper hand, but progressively the advantage switched to the Parliamentarians as Cromwell's army grew in strength, morale and handling. Victory at the Battle of Marston Moor on 2 July 1644 gave the Parliamentarians control of northern England. At the Battle of Naseby on 14 June 1645, Parliament tested out its New Model Army, formed the previous January and commanded by Sir Thomas Fairfax. This was an organized and disciplined conventional body of infantry with a unified command and was a big improvement over the militia and private armies that had been fighting Parliament's corner up until now. This force, and the 'Ironsides' cavalry commanded by Cromwell himself, effectively demolished the Royalist resistance at Naseby. Cromwell subsequently defeated an invasion by a Scottish army in 1648, at Preston on 17–19 August 1648. Charles I was executed in 1649 and, now without their king, the Royalists struggled on in Ireland and Scotland until Cromwell, often showing heightened brutality towards civilian populations, crushed the final resistance in at the Battle of Worcester in September 1651. Cromwell established the Commonwealth, with himself appointed as Lord Protector in 1653 – effectively a dictatorship. He died in 1658 and two years later England restored a monarch, Charles II, to the throne.

In wider Europe, the period from 1689 to 1750 was dominated by a seemingly intractable series of dynastic and imperial wars. Three in particular are known for their scale and destructiveness. The War of the Grand Alliance (1689–97), also called War of the League of Augsburg, was fought between the Bourbon French king Louis XIV and a broad alliance led by England, the United Provinces of the Netherlands and the Habsburg dynasty. Close on its heels, the Spanish War of Succession (1701–14) came from a dispute over who should take the throne of Spain following the death of the childless Charles II (r. 1660–85) in 1700, with England, the Netherlands and Austria again allied against France, who had Spain as an ally. The War of the Austrian Succession (1740–8) was another great European war, one that involved an even larger number of combatants. It was sparked by the death of Holy Roman Emperor Charles VI (r. 1711–40), and Frederick II (r. 1740–86) of Prussia's invasion of Silesia – both events in 1740. This conflict also had a global flavour to it, as France and Britain fought in North America over their respective colonial boundaries. Alongside these struggles we can also add the Great Northern War of 1700–21, in which Sweden's Charles XII (r. 1697–1718) took on Denmark-Norway, Prussia, Saxony-Poland and Russia in the Baltic.

What these conflicts did, to varying extents, was to re-engineer the political map of Europe. France in 1750 was confirmed as the leading state in continental Western Europe, although this ascendancy would be abruptly stopped by Prussia in the Franco-

Prussian War of 1870–1 (see Chapter 4). In the far north of Europe, the Great Northern War resulted in Russian supremacy, establishing itself as new power player in European affairs. This was at the expense of Sweden, which began a steep decline, especially following the death of its warrior king, Charles XII, who was killed in battle at Fredrikshald, Norway, on 30 November 1718.

These conflicts also elevated a fresh crop of talented commanders to fame or notoriety. Alongside individuals such as Charles XII we can place Marshal Tallard of France and Britain's General John Churchill, 1st Duke of Marlborough. The latter indeed ranks as one of Britain's finest military leaders, defeating Tallard at the Battle of Blenheim (13 August 1704), Marshal Villeroi at Ramillies (23 May 1706) and the capable Marshal Villars at Malplaquet (11 September 1709), although the latter was a pyrrhic victory, Marlborough's Dutch-British army taking 55,000 casualties, most due to the excellence of France's artillery and musketry.

The 17th and 18th centuries were truly a time in which warfare changed in its fundamental nature, and some armies and commanders flourished in these conditions, while others sank. In the age that followed (1750–1914), the wheels of change kept turning, however. While the wars of this chapter were of such scope and scale that some challenge the notion that the war of 1914–18 (World War I) was the first global conflict, the world was about to enter a new era, one that saw the beginnings of what we today might call 'total war'.

CHAPTER 4
IMPERIAL AND
REVOLUTIONARY WARFARE

The period from roughly 1750 until the onset of World War I in 1914 inaugurated the age of what we might term 'industrial warfare'. The first 100 years of this era saw only incremental – although some highly significant – changes in tactics, particularly during the Revolutionary and Napoleonic Wars, but from 1850 onwards the world made a series of leaps in weapon technology that fundamentally reconfigured war-making.

By 1750, the practice of warfare had largely settled into closely prescribed tactical limits. On land, a standing professional army, of great size and expense, was a visible pillar of any modern, successful state. These armies were composed of three key elements – infantry, artillery and cavalry – the latter still critical for decisive and fast manoeuvre, while infantry and artillery delivered the lion's share of attrition. Much tactical thought was given to the best way to move and place all these elements in battle. In the realm of the infantry, for example, there was considerable posturing about whether, or when, to deploy infantry units in column or line. 'Column' should not be pictured as a narrow line of troops, snaking thinly towards the enemy. They could actually be wide (indeed wider than they were long), with a front of dozens of men, but still much narrower than the long front-facing line, which would draw up over hundreds of metres, sometimes in ranks as thin as two men deep.

Each formation brought its own set of advantages and disadvantages. The line's advantage was that it presented forward the maximum volume of musket firepower. The very length of a line meant that it was a challenge to turn its flank, and it also helped to reduce casualties – a cannonball hitting an infantry line might only kill two or three men, rather than ploughing on through deeper ranks like skittles. On the downside, the line was a nightmare to control on the forward advance, especially across rough or broken terrain, and it was also vulnerable to cavalry attack. It was for this latter reason that armies became adept at moving from line into square, literally a hollow four-sided infantry box with the infantry on each side of the square presenting their muskets and bayonets outwards. This formation was almost impossible for cavalry to break, although it did make a tantalizingly convenient target for enemy artillery.

The column, meanwhile, had the advantage of speed and concentration of force; think of it as an infantry battering ram, which could be directed at the weakest points of the enemy line. Columns were easier to control, even over difficult terrain, and they could make nimble turns and deviations, unlike the line, which had to perform all manner of complex hinging movements. The compact and solid mass of a column was also better able to withstand cavalry assaults. But it wasn't all good news. Because of its narrower front, the column limited the number of muskets that could be presented at any one time, reducing the formation's firepower. For example, during the Napoleonic Wars, a battalion of 720 men deployed in column had only 240 men who were able to fire their muskets forwards. Columns were also cruelly exposed to artillery fire – and this was an artillery age.

The tactical decisions about column, line or square were muddied by all sorts of factors, including the intervals and linear/

Re-enactors unleash a volley of coordinated musket fire at the re-enactment of the 225th anniversary of the American Continental Army's victory over the British at Yorktown, Virginia, in 1781.

angular relations between formations, the position of the cavalry and artillery, the dimensions and nature of the terrain, and the size of the army. We should note these formations could be expanded until dauntingly huge; at the Battle of Wagram in July 1809, the French marshal Jacques MacDonald (the surname is explained by his father, who came from western Scotland) deployed three infantry divisions (23 battalions) in a vast 8,000-man column. We should also remember that it was not just a case of 'either/or'; master tacticians such as Napoleon, as we shall see, mixed line and column on the battlefield, with telling effect.

Command-and-control, as one might expect in these pre-radio days, was an extreme challenge, relying on flag signals, musical signals from drums and pipes, visible standards and pre-arranged commands, plus the instructions from messengers rushing on to the battlefield clutching instructions from the overall commander, who ideally was positioned on some elevated viewing point. But add the noise, confusion and smoke of the battlefield (black-powder smoke from muskets and cannon could reduce visibility to a matter of mere metres), and nimble tactical responses were often not an option – another reason why formulaic formations were adopted.

Another two key conditions, or at least aspirations, of armies of this age were professionalism and discipline. Serving in the military became a career for many, and there was a steady movement towards meritocratic leadership, albeit one that differed in pace and period according to the national army. (Most of Napoleon's marshals, for example, rose on the basis of merit, giving rise to Napoleon's quote that 'Every French soldier carries a marshal's baton in his knapsack.') States formed armies of monumental size through conscription or voluntary recruitment, but those below officer class were typically the roughest elements of society. Moulding them into an effective fighting force, and one capable of holding formation under air-scorching fire, was typically the result of cruellest discipline. In both army and naval service, infractions were discouraged by a spectrum of punishments, ranging from simple punishment duties through to flogging and execution. Add violent death and injury in battle, poor food, dire sanitation, and the presence of disease (which on campaign invariably killed more than battle), and the life of a soldier on campaign was generally not a pleasant one, the hardships borne by men of an age for whom stoicism was a default setting.

Types of Cannon Ammunition

Prior to the development of breech-loading rifled artillery and explosive shells in the second half of the 19th century, the primary types of cannon ammunition were as follows:

Round shot – The most common type, round shot was the classic solid cannonball. It could be used as anti-materiel ordnance to destroy walls, defences etc., and also as an anti-personnel shell. In infantry battles, the round shot was usually fired so that it struck the ground in front of the infantry ranks, then skipped on through the packed soldiers in a low, destructive arc. In naval warfare, round shot was sometimes heated over flames before being fired; this 'hot shot' would embed in the enemy ship and start a fire.

Canister – Essentially a giant shotgun shell, canister consisted of a thin steel can packed with small (c.25mm/1in diameter) irons balls surrounded by sawdust. When the shell was fired, the powder charge ruptured the can, leaving the balls to fly on in a wide, destructive pattern. It was specifically designed for anti-personnel use.

Grapeshot – Grapeshot worked in a similar way to canister, with multiple shot balls packed in a geometric pattern into a canvas bag, to give a more predictable dispersion on firing. Grapeshot found particular utility in naval warfare, for cutting rigging, sails and destroying naval equipment.

 An artillery canister round for a 12-pounder cannon, which contained a total of 37 pieces of cast-iron shot for a devastating shotgun-like effect on enemy ranks.

Exploding shell – Before the age of high-explosive shells, hollow round shot was filled with gunpowder and shrapnel and fitted with a burning fuse, cut to the desired burn duration. The fuse was lit by the propelling charge upon firing, and when the shell exploded it would generate lethal shrapnel in the vicinity.

In naval use, other types of shell included bar shot and chain shot, which featured double balls or weighted ends attached, respectively, by a solid bar or a length of chain. These munitions were designed to scythe through sails and rigging.

THE SEVEN YEARS' WAR

The Seven Years' War was termed 'the first world war' by none other than British Prime Minister Winston Churchill. This perception has some justification. Fought between 1756 and 1763, the war had multiple theatres – Europe, the Americas, West Africa, India and the Philippines – and dragged in most European powers plus many combatants beyond.

In many ways, it makes more sense to view the Seven Years' War as several related but largely separate conflicts, unified by the combatants and also the international war between naval powers. The Seven Years' War in the North American theatre is known more regionally as the French and Indian War. By the middle part of the 18th century, France was largely in control of Canada (known as 'New France'), while the eastern seaboard of what would become the USA was governed by the 13 colonies of Great Britain. Friction between these two powers, and also with the Native Americans whom European colonialism attempted to overwrite, was long-standing, with the French and British already in a state of semi-conflict along the frontier region. Fighting began in earnest in 1754 around what is today Pittsburgh, when skirmishing between the two sides flared out into more substantial battle. Notably, the officer at the centre of the initial fighting was none other than George Washington, at this time 22 years old, later to become the commander of American rebel forces during the War of Independence, and then the first president of the USA. At this time, however, he was a commissioned officer in the Virginia Militia. As the fighting grew, Washington was appointed aide-de-camp to General Edward Braddock, the British commander-in-chief in North America.

At first, it was the British who were on the back foot, suffering a particularly embarrassing defeat on the Monongahela River in July 1755, during a British expedition to capture the French-held

Fort Duquesne. In 1756, the British formally declared war on France, and in 1757 supported Prussia's efforts to fight France in Continental Europe. Britain, under a new prime minister, William Pitt, began to pour troops and resources into North America, also reimbursing the American colonies for the cost of raising troops.

This investment in the theatre began to pay off. In 1758, a reinvigorated British/colonial army secured victories at Louisbourg, Fort Frontenac and Fort Duquesne. Then, in September 1759, came the jewel in the crown, when 8,000 troops under General James Wolfe captured Quebec, doing so after scaling the 50 m (164 ft)-high Heights of Abraham to make a surprise night attack. In 1760, Montreal fell, and France's hold over North America was fatally weakened.

Over the Atlantic in Europe, the Seven Years' War was in many ways a continuation of the earlier War of Austrian Succession, and began over the contested status of Silesia, which had been given to Frederick the Great of Prussia in the Treaty of Aix-La-Chapelle. In August 1756, Frederick's Prussian army invaded Saxony, triggering a conflict in which Prussia and Britain squared off against France, Austria, Russia and several other states.

In the early battles of the war, Prussia struggled to gain advantage. Frederick took Leipzig and Dresden, then besieged Prague in Bohemia, but was compelled to raise the siege after his first major defeat against an Austrian relief army at Kolín in June 1757. A further defeat followed against the Russians at Gross-Jägersdorf on 30 July, but then came a landmark series of Prussian victories. At Rossbach on 5 November, the Prussians demolished a Franco-Austrian army of c.41,000 men with just 21,000 of their own, Frederick outmanoeuvring and outgunning his opponents to achieve victory in just 90 minutes, sustaining 548 casualties to 10,150 on the Franco-Austrian side. The Austrians winced under another brutal defeat at Leuthen in Silesia just a month later, on

6 December, causing the Austrians to withdraw to Bohemia. On 1 August 1759, a combined British and Hanoverian army, led by Prince Ferdinand of Brunswick, also took the field at Minden, using an infantry charge and the concentrated fire of mobile artillery to break the French lines around the town. Although much hard fighting and some setbacks lay ahead for Frederick and his allies, the Anglo-Prussian alliance prevailed against their enemies, although Prussia was paying an especially high price in lives to do so.

During this war, fighting flared up in many places around the world, especially if we include the naval theatres. At Quiberon Bay off the coast of southern France on 20 November 1759, for example, a Royal Navy squadron under Sir Edward Hawke defeated a gathering French invasion force, destined for England, with eight French ships either lost or captured during the battle across squally seas. Far distant from Europe, at Plassey in Bengal, India, on 23 June 1757, a British force (regular army and troops of the East India Company) just 3,000 strong defeated 55,000 troops – including a unit of French artillery with 50 guns – under the Nawab of Bengal, partly through Clive's vigorous tactics and partly because many of the Nawab's officers had covertly switched their loyalty to the British. This victory secured Bengal for the British, and within 100 years they ruled over all of India.

The Seven Years' War concluded in 1763 with two treaties signed in February that year. France lost all of North America east of the Mississippi to Britain, while in mainland Europe the status quo of 1748 was essentially restored. The most important outcome of the war, however, was that Britain was now seen as the world's dominant naval power, while Prussian might on land appeared unchallenged.

AMERICAN WAR OF INDEPENDENCE

The American War of Independence (1775–83) was a startling corrective to Britain's sense of military confidence following the

Seven Years' War. By 1775, the year of the war's outbreak, the population of colonial North America had reached 4 million, many of whom were beginning to resent taxations and duties imposed by distant British masters. Rioting and demonstrative acts of protest, including the dumping of a cargo of British-monopolized tea in the harbour at Boston in December 1773 – the so-called Boston Tea Party – caused the British to act militarily in response. A sortie by General Thomas Gage, the British commander-in-chief, to seize arms and gunpowder in Middlesex County, Massachusetts, in April 1775 led to shock defeats at the hands of rebel troops at Lexington and Concord. A soberingly pyrrhic victory at Breed's Hill and Bunker Hill around Boston was a temporary reprieve for the British, and they were subsequently forced to evacuate the city by sea in March 1776. Scalded into more intensive action, the British poured in reinforcements – in September 1776, General William Howe, the new commander-in-chief of British forces in America, landed in New York with 30,000 reinforcements, with which he subsequently took New York City and Philadelphia. By this time, the rebels had formed a Continental Army, led by none other the George Washington.

There are some notions about the American War of Independence that need to be clarified. The first is that this was not a conflict of 'Americans vs British', but was rather part civil war, part colonial war. Many American militia forces fought as loyalist units for the British, and Native Americans were found on both sides. The war also came to have an international dimension. The British war effort was supported by some 16,000 Hessians – German auxiliary troops – although Germans were found in limited numbers on the rebel side as well. More significantly, in September–October 1777, a major British force under General John Burgoyne, invading down from Canada in an attempt to cut off rebels in New England, took progressively serious losses until, on 17 October, the survivors were compelled to surrender to the Americans. This British defeat was a turning point in the war, not least because it led to France, Spain and Holland allying themselves to the American cause, particularly providing naval support. Indeed, the naval aspect of the War of Independence was fought far and wide, with an engagement between the nascent Continental Navy and the Royal Navy even taking place in the North Sea off England in September 1779.

Another myth about the war is that the Americans fought *primarily* with unconventional 'guerrilla'-type tactics – sniping, manoeuvring and skirmishing – tactics that the regimented lines of British 'redcoats' struggled to deal with. This notion does have a significant element of truth. In several battles and campaigns, the Americans did apply more open and flexible tactics to inflict a rolling attrition upon the British units. At the Battle of Cowpens (17 January 1781), for example, some 2,000 Americans under Brigadier Daniel Morgan made a double-envelopment of 1,000 British troops under Colonel Sir Banastre Tarleton. Morgan's troops included 500 sharpshooters known as 'Morgan's Riflemen', experts at precision fire with rifled muskets. These men, and others, relentlessly hewed down the British ranks, particularly targeting officers. In the end, only 200 of the British force escaped. Yet there were also many conventional battles, as Washington and his commanders worked to bring the Continental Army up to professional battlefield order. This was not always easy given the Americans' shortage of weapons, gunpowder, money, food, clothing and medicine. Note that the Continental Army was supported by a large number of local and private militias, of variable quality and resources.

From 1780, the British war effort was mainly concentrated in the central and southern parts of the theatre. Both sides took their victories and defeats, but generally speaking the Americans could sustain the war effort better than the British, and the colonial position became ever weaker. Then, in autumn 1781, a British garrison at the port town of Yorktown, Virginia, was trapped by a Franco-American army from the land and a French fleet offshore. Having been squeezed back into less defendable perimeters, under frequent artillery fire, and with no relief in sight, the British commander at Yorktown, General Charles Cornwallis, surrendered his troops to Washington on 19 October.

It was this defeat that psychologically and practically sealed Britain's defeat in the American War of Independence, and in 1783 the war ended with the Treaty of Paris. Although the Declaration of Independence had been signed back on 4 July 1776, the USA was now truly a free and sovereign nation.

FRENCH REVOLUTIONARY AND NAPOLEONIC WARS

The French Revolution of 1789 began a chain of events that not only transformed French and indeed European politics, but also altered the core model of inter-state warfare. It also provided the conditions for the rise of arguably the greatest military commander in history – Napoleon Bonaparte – who for more than a decade proved almost invincible in battle, at least on land, until his forces suffered a series of spectacular defeats between 1812 and 1815. Here, we will provide a brief arc of both the Revolutionary and Napoleonic Wars, before reflecting upon why the French army proved such a strategic and tactical juggernaut for so long, and against so many enemies.

The French Revolution of 1789, which overthrew the monarchy and aristocracy, may have been a moment of national upheaval, but it sent shockwaves through wider Europe. Fearing a contagion of anti-monarchism, many European states began squaring up to France, and in April 1792 France declared war on Austria and Prussia. Despite the chaotic and disorganized nature of the revolutionary army at this stage (it had lost many of its officers, who were often of noble birth), it was sizeable and highly motivated, with an excellent artillery arm, and it defeated the Prussians at the Battle of Valmy on 20 September 1792. Shortly after this, France declared itself a Republic (another scandalous political decision in the eyes of European rulers) and then, in January 1793, King Louis XVI was executed.

These events triggered what is known as the War of the First Coalition, in which Germany, Austria, Prussia, Great Britain, Spain, Portugal, the Netherlands, Sardinia, Naples and various Italian states gathered themselves collectively against France. This was the first of six such coalitions against which France would fight between 1793 and 1813, the composition of the alliances varying over time. For the most part, France was almost unstoppable on the battlefield, disproportionately winning more battles than it lost.

In 1793, the French Committee of Public Safety declared a *levée en masse* – a national conscription programme that gathered a vast citizen army of amateur soldiers. Here was a new model for warfare, the idea that all citizens were involved in the defence of the nation. The conscription law stated that: 'Young men shall fight; married men shall make weapons and transport supplies; women will make tents and clothes and will serve in the hospitals; children will turn old linen into bandages; old men will be carried into public squares to make inspiring speeches for the soldiers, to preach hatred against kings, and to declare the unity of the republic.' This was a vision, in effect, of *total war*, in which all the resources of society were directed to military victory. Under the reforms of Lazare Nicolas Carnot – known as the 'Organizer of Victory' – this unwieldy force took shape, discipline and administrative efficiency, which combined with its generally high morale and excellent leadership made it a war-winning force.

Although due credit for these victories must be given to the many marshals who commanded French corps – towering figures such as Louis-Nicolas Davout, Jean Lannes and Nicolas Soult –

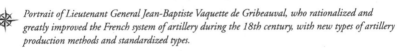

Portrait of Lieutenant General Jean-Baptiste Vaquette de Gribeauval, who rationalized and greatly improved the French system of artillery during the 18th century, with new types of artillery production methods and standardized types.

A portrait of Napoleon Bonaparte. He appears youthful in this artwork, and he certainly demonstrated an accelerated ability for achievement – he was appointed Emperor of France at just 34 years old.

there is one man in particular who made France, for a time, the undisputed military superpower of Europe: Napoleon Buonaparte.

Born in Corsica in 1769, Napoleon undertook a military education in France, specializing in artillery, and distinguished himself to the new French regime by suppressing revolts on the streets of Paris in 1795, then through a series of lighting victories in Italy, as commander of the Army of Italy in 1796–7. His forward momentum continued when he subsequently led an expeditionary force against the British in Egypt, capturing Alexandria and Cairo in short order. Admiral Horatio Nelson's victory over the French invasion fleet at Aboukir Bay, also known as the Battle of the Nile, in August 1798 trapped the French army in North Africa and limited the campaign. Napoleon, however, slipped back to France in August 1799, leading a *coup d'état* that brought him political power as First Consul. The subsequent military brilliance he demonstrated, plus his shrewd handling of France's new politics, led to him being declared Consul for Life in 1802 then, in 1804, the Emperor of France. The country had gone effectively from being a republic to a dictatorship.

Napoleon's life and military campaigns resist quick summary. An indicator of his military genius, however, is that he personally led some 70 battles in his lifetime, against the most powerful states in Europe, and with eight exceptions (some of them crucial, nonetheless) he won almost all of them. Landmark battles include Marengo (1800), Austerlitz (1805), Jena (1806), Wagram (1809) and Borodino (1812), but the list could go on. These clashes were frequently of huge scale; the Battle of Wagram, for example, fought north-east of Vienna between the French and the Austrians, brought 250,000 men to the field of battle, where they fought over two days (5–6 July) and at a cost of *c*.80,000 dead.

There are a multitude of reasons why Napoleon achieved the level of victories he did. Personally, he was an aggressive and intelligent commander with a bias towards fast offensive action – his enemies were frequently wrong-footed when Napoleon's troops made blistering long-distance marches to gain a manoeuvre advantage. He was skilled at spotting weak points in the enemy battle lines, and talented at applying his infantry and cavalry at the right moment. He was innovative in his battle formations, applying the *ordre mixte* – brigades in alternating lines of column and line, to combine firepower and movement – to good effect. He moved his corps in *battaillon carré*, positioning his divisions so that they could turn, move and attack in almost any direction at a moment's notice. Napoleon had the advantage of an excellent French artillery arm; as an artilleryman himself, he had the technical knowledge to wield it effectively. His superb memory meant that he also had a decent eye for logistics, although most of his campaigns relied upon his army foraging off the land around them.

Yet despite his brilliance, Napoleon could be outfought and ultimately, defeated, and he could make mistakes. His first major land defeat came at the Battle of Aspern-Essling in May 1809, and his war in the Iberian Peninsula (1807–14), in which France faced both guerrilla warfare and an Anglo-Portuguese army under the command of the talented Sir Arthur Wellesley, Duke of Wellington, remained a draining thorn in the side of the French war effort. France was further never able to take control of the seas from a confident Royal Navy.

In June 1812, Napoleon began one of his most disastrous campaigns, when he led an army of 600,000 men on an invasion of Russia. Although the French reached Moscow, defeating the Russian army at Borodino on the way, the capital was largely deserted and stripped of supplies, and much of it burned down in a subsequent fire. Napoleon's exhausted army therefore had to retreat hundreds of kilometres back to the West, through the sub-zero horrors of a Russian winter and preyed on constantly by raiding Russians. Only

20,000 of his men made it back. Critically weakened, Napoleon's army was subsequently defeated in the massive Battle of Leipzig (16–19 October 1813), the largest battle in Europe before World War I – a defeat that led to Napoleon's abdication and exile to the Italian island of Elba in April 1814.

This was not to be Napoleon's final act, however. In 1815, Napoleon fled Elba with his bodyguard, returned to France, and took the position of Emperor once again, drawing a loyal army to him. However, his return to the world stage was emphatically quashed by an Anglo-Prussian army – the British forces led by Wellington, and the Prussians by Field Marshal Gebhard Leberecht von Blücher – at the Battle of Waterloo on 18 June 1815. This time there would be no escape for Napoleon; he was imprisoned on the remote South Atlantic island of St Helena, where he died in 1821.

STEEL, STEAM AND FIRE

Beyond the Napoleonic Wars, the 19th century was a period in which warfare underwent another of those periodic leaps forwards, primarily in terms of technology and weaponry, but with critical knock-on effects in tactical and strategic thinking. At the heart of these changes was a revolution in firepower. The flintlock system, having served armies relatively well for more than two centuries, was showing its age and limitations. From the 1820s began a series of fundamental technical steps forwards in firearm design. First came the percussion cap, *c.*1814 – a small metal cap filled with an impact-detonated chemical compound – which eventually came to replace the flint as a far more reliable ignition system on infantry weapons. (Note that with all these inventions, it often took considerable time for the invention to become widespread in use, particularly among armed forces who had to produce and purchase new weapons in large volumes, plus invest in associated training.) In 1836, the American Samuel Colt patented a revolving handgun, a cap-and-ball weapon with five chambers, giving five rapid shots with five trigger pulls in a single weapon. In 1846, the Frenchman Claude-Etienne Minié invented the Minié ball for use with rifled muskets.

Rifling – spiral grooves cut inside the bore of a firearm – imparted gyroscopic spin stabilization to a bullet, with superb improvements in accuracy when compared to smoothbore weapons. Rifled weapons had been around for centuries, but were relatively rare compared to smoothbores because they were slower to load; the bullet had to be of a tight fit to ensure that it engraved on to the rifling during firing, and this slowed the loading times. The Minié ball, however, was designed to drop quickly into the rifle, then its base expanded on firing to grip the rifling. With this invention (admittedly it stood on the shoulders of others), rifled weapons became more commonplace on the battlefield; indeed, they would entirely replace smoothbores during the second half of the 19th century.

But the defining change in firearms design was the invention of the unitary cartridge – meaning that powder, primer (the means of ignition) and bullet/ball were contained in a single, handy unit, loaded via the breech of the weapon, not the muzzle. The importance of this invention, which began in Paris in 1808 with the Swiss gunsmith Jean Samuel Pauly, working with French gunsmith François Prélat, but was developed by others, cannot be overstated. Breech-loading, unitary cartridge weapons began to emerge in the 1830s, at first with cardboard and paper cartridges but later with metal cases. These cartridges, allied to new systems of magazine feed and loading action, and with bullets accurized by rifling, produced new generations of firearms that were fast-firing, accurate over ranges of hundreds of metres and superbly reliable. In 1841, the Prussians adopted the Dreyse Needle Gun as their standard-issue infantry weapon, a bolt-action rifle that could fire

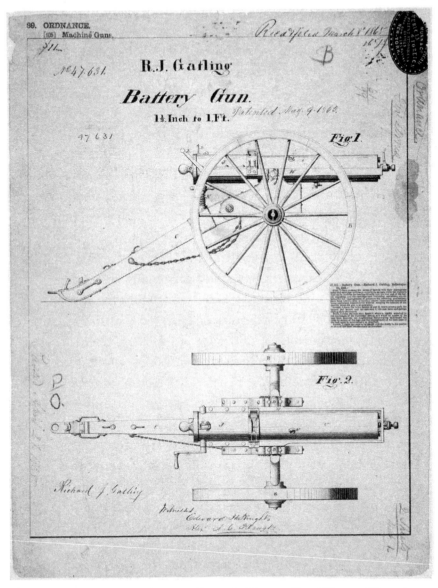

A patent drawing for the Gatling Gun or 'Battery Gun'. Later models could fire up to 900 rounds per minute, although the rate of fire depended on how fast the operator could crank it.

six or more rounds per minute, the absence of muzzle loading also meaning that the soldier could fire his weapon from behind cover or in the prone position. By the end of the century, all the world's modern armies were equipped with bolt-action rifles, far better than the Dreyse, such as the German Mauser Gewehr 98 and the British Lee–Enfield. Furthermore, modern 'smokeless' high-performance propellants had replaced traditional gunpowder, with a transformative effect on firearms power and reliability.

The breech-loading, cartridge-fed firearm reached its apogee in the 19th century with the invention of the first machine guns. The landmarks in this regard were the hand-cranked, multi-barrel Gatling gun, invented by American Richard Gatling and patented in 1862; and the recoil-powered, belt-fed Maxim Gun of 1884, firing up to 600 rpm. But artillery had also transformed itself by this time. Rifled, breech-loading artillery pieces made their first appearance in the 1830s, and steadily replaced the muzzle-loading cannon as the century progressed. Like their smaller firearms relations, breech-loading artillery was fast-loading (it also adopted unitary ammunition for its smaller field pieces) – a well-oiled crew of a French Matériel de 75mm Mle 1897 field gun, for example, could fire 15–30 rpm at burst rate. Ranges were constantly extended, so that a typical turn-of-the-century howitzer could reach out to a maximum range of 7–10 km (4.4–6 miles). Moreover, artillery pieces in the very late 19th and early 20th centuries now fired shells filled with high-explosive compounds, making artillery a weapon with true 'area effects' – i.e. destruction over a wide area.

In land warfare, all these inventions served to make the battlefield an increasingly lethal space. To be exposed, immobile and visible invited destruction. In incremental response, infantry tactics began to focus more on open formations and faster manoeuvre rather than defiant lines of close-packed soldiers. Uniforms became less ostentatious and more muted in colour; khaki, olive-drab and field grey, and subtle variations thereof, became near standard garb by the end of the century. Because of the risk of precision fires and high-explosive ordnance, infantry also became more adept at digging defensive trenches and establishing field fortifications; here was the beginning of the trench warfare that would define World War I.

Maxim Gun

The Maxim Gun offered levels of infantry firepower in the late 19th century that would still be respected on the battlefield today. It was invented by American-born Briton Hiram Stevens Maxim in 1884. Maxim was actually a general inventor – other inventions include a mousetrap, a steam pump and hair-curling irons – but he was apparently inspired to develop a weapon after a business associate told him to 'Hang your chemistry and electricity! If you want to make a pile of money, invent something that will enable these Europeans to cut each others' throats with greater facility.' This he did in the Maxim Gun. The revolutionary principle behind the weapon was that it used the force of recoil to power the gun automatically through its cycle of operation; all the user had to do to fire the belt-fed gun at cyclical rate of 550–600 rpm was to hold down the trigger – one of Maxim's early marketing demonstrations was to cut down a large tree with machine-gun fire. The Maxim Gun changed warfare profoundly, giving a two- or three-man machine-gun team the firepower of an entire company of rifle-armed soldiers.

In the realm of communications, warfare also began its advance towards the modern era. The advent of the electric telegraph and cable, once it was applied to warfare, meant that inter-theatre and ultimately international communications became possible, compressing the timeline of strategic decision-making from many days or weeks (the time it took to carry a message by foot, horse or ship) to mere minutes. At the frontline, the increasing use of field telephones in the late 19th century augured the end of visual communications such as semaphore and heliographs.

At the strategic level, one of the most significant non-military creations of the industrial revolution was the perfection of the steam train and the concomitant web-like spread of the railway network across Europe, the Americas and eventually the world. Railways provided the ability to move thousands of troops and tons of supplies quickly and in coordinated fashion to distant battlefields, without the biological hassles that came with horse and foot movement. On par with the impact of railway, and also related to steam technology, was the invention of the steamship. Coal-burning steamships, made from steel rather than wood, were crossing the world's seas and oceans in the 1820s and 30s. 'Ironclad' warships began to appear in the second half of the 19th century. Free from sail, and capable of global voyages (at least in frequent steps between coaling ports), these warships could now manoeuvre with near unlimited freedom, and they took on heavy breech-loading artillery, often mounted in revolving turrets. Shipborne armour also became more substantial, to improve the survivability of warships against modern high-explosive shells, and more sophisticated fire-direction instruments meant gun battles could be fought at opposite edges of the horizon.

The apogee of warship development during this period was the dreadnought battleships of the early 20th century. These potent vessels, bristling with heavy guns of 305 mm (12 in) calibre or greater, displacing more than 20,000 long tons, and with complements of 700-plus officers and men, were giants of the seas, the vanguard of national fleets. We should note, however, that the 19th century also saw the first crude steps in a type of naval warship that would ultimately be the undoing of the battleship: the submarine.

Here arrived the age of 'industrial' warfare. War was now not just fought on the battlefield, but also in the factories and industrial plants (also steam-powered), which were capable through standardized manufacturing processes of churning out weapons and military materiel in unprecedented volumes. Add the rise of the internal combustion engine, which alongside civilian transport also produced history's first armoured vehicles, and the old ways of war were destined for rapid obsolescence.

MAJOR REGIONAL WARS, 1850-1914

The period from 1850 to 1914 is another complex one in the history of warfare. To acquire a sense of how the changes above affected the actual field of battle, we direct our focus to three of the major conflicts of this period – the American Civil War, the Franco-Prussian War and the Russo-Japanese War – before taking an overview of the multitude of 'small wars' that flourished in this belligerent age.

The American Civil War (1861–65) began in April 1861, when Confederate artillery fired on Union positions at Fort Sumter in Charleston Harbor. ('Confederates' refer to the army of the Southern states that wanted to secede from the USA, while the 'Union' army was that of the federal government.) What began as a dispute over slavery and the differences between Northern and Southern economies became a conflagration that killed more than 620,000 people. The war was fought across most of eastern and central USA, that territory divided into several sub-theatres. On paper, and indeed in reality, the North held many advantages compared to the South. Its population was greater, which in turn led it to form a conscript Union Army of 2.8 million men – the South had 1.1 million. The North had far larger industrial capacity to produce essential war materiel, plus it rested on the distribution advantages of more extensive road and rail networks. The South struggled continually to meet the needs of its army, short of weapons, gunpowder, uniforms and even shoes. The situation was made worse for the South in that the North had naval supremacy during the war, and thus was able to impose a blockade of Southern ports.

Yet despite the evident disparity between the two sides, the Union struggled for four long years to achieve its victory, against a Southern army short on equipment but high on motivation. Both sides embarked on offensive campaigning, which produced a continual series of pitched battles and accompanying attrition on both sides. In 1861–3, the Confederates, particularly under their outstanding commander Robert E. Lee, often had the Union on the back foot with victories such as First Bull Run (21 July 1861), the Seven Days Battles (25 June–1 July 1862), Fredericksburg (13 December 1862) and Chancellorsville (30 April–6 May 1863). But with every Confederate win came more bodies added to a pile of unsustainable losses; it was notable that after many battlefield wins the Confederates generally did not have the strength to make a pursuit operation. Then, on 1–3 July 1863, Lee's Army of Northern Virginia suffered a grievous body blow at the Battle of Gettysburg. This defeat, inflicted by General George G. Meade's Army of the Potomac, cost the Confederates 28,000 casualties; the Union suffered 23,000 casualties, making Gettysburg the bloodiest battle on US soil.

The defeat at Gettysburg, and the fall of Vicksburg – a Confederate stronghold under siege since May – on 4 July, began the downfall of the Confederate war effort. Union General Ulysses S. Grant, commander-in-chief from 1864, imposed an unswerving campaign of attrition on the South, although the Confederates remained formidable until the end, especially in defensive

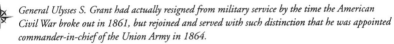 *General Ulysses S. Grant had actually resigned from military service by the time the American Civil War broke out in 1861, but rejoined and served with such distinction that he was appointed commander-in-chief of the Union Army in 1864.*

positions. On 9 April 1865, however, Lee's shattered army was forced to surrender, and the last capitulation of Confederate forces came the following June.

The American Civil war straddled the old and the new. Alongside traditional smoothbore cannon, ripples of musket fire and screaming bayonet charges were more modern forms of warfare: use of repeating rifles such as the Sharps; sophisticated fieldwork defences with emplaced artillery; the extensive use of black-powder landmines; the first ironclad 'monitor' warships fighting each other at the Battle of Hampton Roads (8–9 March 1862); and the first combat missions of early submarines, the Confederate submarine *H.L. Hunley* sinking the sloop USS *Housatonic* in Charleston Harbor on 17 February 1864. Modern war-making in no way made conflict more sanitary, however; the country's civilian population suffered as much as the soldiers on the battlefield during these terrible four years.

An ocean away from North America, the Franco-Prussian War (1870–1) was very different from the American Civil War in strategic context – it was sparked by a dispute between Prussia and France over the vacant Spanish throne – but it saw some similar ingredients in terms of the combat, as well as notable contrasts. One immediate point of interest is that both sides were now armed with bolt-action rifles: the French with the 11 mm Chassepot and the Prussians with the Dreyse Needle Gun (the French rifle was actually the superior weapon). The French also brought to the field the *mitrailleuse*, a 25-barrel 'volley gun' – a progenitor of the machine gun – mounted on a wheeled carriage like an artillery piece. Both sides also had modern breech-loading field and siege artillery, although in this war the Prussian pieces and their gunnery techniques had the advantage.

It was the French who declared war on Prussia, on 19 July 1870. The French Emperor, Napoleon III, was highly confident of victory, yet from the outset it would be the Prussians, under their commander-in-chief General Helmut von Moltke, who took the upper hand. A key advantage of the Prussian Army lay in its highly efficient and professional general staff, which meticulously and intelligently planned Prussian mobilization and deployment. In particular, it used Europe's railway system to optimal advantage, shifting large numbers of troops to key points on the frontlines with a speed and coordination that the French could not match.

The French consequently found themselves continually outmanoeuvred. The left wing of the French Army was pushed back into the fortress of Metz, where they were essentially trapped until the end of the war. On 1–2 September 1870, a vast engagement at Sedan, which involved 120,000 French troops and 200,000 Germans, saw the French defeated with massive losses, mainly due to the unrelenting slashes of German artillery fire, which had a particularly cruel effect on spirited French cavalry charges. The French defence now broke apart, and Paris surrendered on 28 January 1871. The war confirmed Prussia as the supreme power in Continental Europe, while equally demonstrating the emasculation of France as a military power. Planning, efficient mobilization and artillery – the latter would become known as the 'king of battles' – now decided the outcome of warfare rather than national spirit.

The Russo-Japanese War (1904–5) perfectly represents the state warfare had reached just prior to the onset of World War I in 1914. It also shows both sides struggling to understand the full significance of the tactical and technological changes, an intellectual wrestling that arguably would not be fully resolved until the last two years of the following world war.

The war's origins lay in Japan's desire to quash Russian military expansionism in China and Manchuria, which if unchecked would have given Russia a strategic dominance in East Asia. A key objective for the Japanese was to neutralize the strategically important Russian-occupied Port Arthur on the Manchurian coast. On the night of 8–9 February 1904, Japan launched a major naval and amphibious operation against the port, where Russia's Pacific Squadron was anchored. Historians have noted that the opening move of this attack – a surprise attack by ten torpedo-armed destroyers against the anchored Russian fleet – hints at the tactic used against the US Pacific fleet in Pearl Harbor in 1941. Although this initial assault was not decisively successful, Port Arthur was placed under a siege that lasted until January 1905. The combat was not like the sieges of the 19th century. Machine guns were in heavy use for both offence and defence; they inflicted a particularly withering cost on Japanese assaults. Trenches' positions, guarded by barbed wire, proliferated, and were fought over using small arms and hand grenades. There is also evidence that the Japanese used poison gas to support some of their attacks.

Carl von Clausewitz

Carl von Clausewitz (1780–1831) was a Prussian general whose theories of warfare came to be highly influential in Western military philosophy, and remain so today. Following service in the Napoleonic Wars, von Clausewitz worked in the Military Academy in Berlin, where he wrote his famous work, *Vom Kriege* (On War). In this work, Clausewitz reflected on the nature of conflict, arguing against the notion that conflict could be reduced to reason and pointing to the role of chance, emotion and 'friction' – the inevitable problematization of even the simplest plans – in determining the outcomes of war. Clausewitz's phrase 'War is the continuation of politics by other means' is one of the most famous encapsulations of conflict in history.

The Russians held out at Port Arthur until their surrender in January 1905, by which time they had suffered 40,000 casualties. The Japanese had actually taken 60,000 casualties during the battle, a greater loss, but nevertheless the Japanese settled into the groove of victory. In Manchuria, the Japanese won battles at Fuhsien and Liaoyang in 1904 and in February–March 1905 won the immense three-week Battle of Mukden, in which some 600,000 men fought. The war had equally impressive clashes at sea, including one of the first big fleet actions between modern battleships. This battle, fought in the Tsushima Strait on 27–28 May, was conducted on a grand scale – the Japanese had four battleships and 27 cruisers vs 11 Russian battleships and 20 other assorted warships. The skilled Japanese admiral, Tōgō Heihachiro, completely outmanoeuvred and outgunned the Russian fleet, however, (the Japanese warships had superior speed, firepower and standards of gunnery training) and sank 21 Russian ships, capturing six others. Given the scale of its repeated defeats, Russia withdrew from Manchuria shortly after.

The Russo-Japanese War was studied carefully by European military leaders in its aftermath, as it formed an early blueprint of the modern way of war, both at land and sea. Artillery was confirmed as the decisive arm, aided by new practices such as having forward observers control artillery fire at beyond visual range using a direct field telephone link to the batteries. In infantry warfare, the machine gun changed the infantry experience profoundly, and would also drive some of the final nails into the coffin of mounted horse cavalry. This battle pointed to an emerging truth: victory would generally go to the side that won the battle for fire superiority.

SMALL WARS

In addition to the major conflicts studied in this chapter, there were a plethora of conflicts fought elsewhere around the world of varying magnitudes, too many to list here, let alone analyze. Britain, for example, reached the peak of its imperial strength during Queen Victoria's reign (1837–1901), and by the early 20th century the British Empire covered almost a quarter of the world's land mass. Inevitably, therefore, Britain found itself involved in numerous colonial struggles around the world, especially in Africa, the Middle East and India. It also fought a major war, allied with France and the Ottoman Turks, against the Russians in the Crimea between 1853 and 1856, the conflict sparked by Russian expansionism as the Ottoman Empire weakened. During the war, a new generation of British soldiers experienced some of the largest engagements since the Napoleonic Wars, with names such as Alma, Inkerman, Balaclava and Sebastopol going down in regimental histories. The Battle of Balaclava on 25 October 1864 was the battle in which the Light Brigade of cavalry, commanded by Lieutenant-General James Thomas Brudenell, the 7th Earl of Cardigan, made its bloodily futile charge uphill against a battery of Russian guns, later to be immortalized in Alfred, Lord Tennyson's narrative poem 'The Charge of the Light Brigade'. The conflict cost half a million lives before peace terms were agreed. It did, however, spur the modernization of several military practices, such as improvements in military medicine (pioneered by British nurse Florence Nightingale) and the use of telegraph communications. It was also the first conflict to be covered significantly by war journalists, and includes some of the earliest examples of war photography.

In most cases of the smaller conflicts, Britain had complete technological superiority over indigenous peoples, including powerful lever-action rifles such as the .577/450 Martini–Herny and Maxim Guns, which inflicted an awful toll on enemies armed primarily with spear, shield and sword. But the scale of the empire meant that many British forces found themselves fighting isolated battles against numerically superior enemies. During the Anglo-Zulu War of 1879, for example, more than 1,600 British troops were slaughtered by 22,000 Zulu warriors at the Battle of Isandhlwana in Natal, South Africa, on 22 January. The same dreadful outcome almost occurred at nearby Rorke's Drift on 22–23 January, but here just 149 men fought off 4,000 Zulus in a magisterial defensive action, which was often conducted hand to hand. In the Boer Wars (1880–1 and 1899–1902), the British Army fought a very different enemy, southern African Boers, mostly hardened farmers with a talent for accurate shooting, skilled horsemanship and a guerrilla-style of warfare that the British found hard to counter. Only Britain's greater economic resources and the imposition of harsh measures on the civilian population – including the use of concentration camps – eventually brought the Boers to surrender in 1902.

Other lively theatres for Britain's 'small wars' were India and what is today Afghanistan. In the latter, Britain suffered an epic military disaster, when in 1842 a British column of 16,000 people (4,500 soldiers and the rest civilians) attempted to march through winter from Kabul to Jalalabad and were destroyed over seven days by predatory attacks from Afghan tribesmen. Such was the extent of the catastrophe that only one British soldier and a few Indian sepoys actually reached Jalalabad. In India, Britain fought several regional wars before its colony was secure, specifically the First (1845–6) and Second (1848–9) Sikh Wars and the Indian Rebellion in 1857–8, which included the six-month siege of British-held Lucknow by Indian forces, the relief of which (achieved in November 1857) became a cause célèbre in British society at the time.

Away from the British imperial territories, the remainder of the world also knew little prolonged peace. The USA spilled blood in numerous campaigns within its territories against the unfortunate Native Americans, who were steadily defeated in battle or squeezed into reservations. Following the annexation of Texas from Mexico in 1845, the two-year Mexican–American War (1846–8) ended in

American troops raise their helmets in celebration as they receive news of the surrender of Spanish forces in Santiago de Cuba in 1898, one of the final acts in the Spanish–American War.

a defeat for Mexico and the territorial expansion of the USA in the south and south-west. At the end of the century, the USA fought the more widespread Spanish–American War of 1898, a conflict that brought US campaign victories in the Philippines, Cuba and elsewhere. During the intervening years, many wars were fought in South America, liberating the nations from Spanish rule, although in their place came many other civil and state wars. The Paraguayan War of 1865 to 1870, for example, was Latin America's bloodiest conflict, fought between Paraguay and an alliance of Argentina, Brazil and Uruguay. This horrific war resulted in the deaths of about 40 per cent of the nation of Paraguay, which was utterly defeated.

The 19th and early 20th centuries, as we have seen, demonstrated once again humanity's seemingly natural instincts for generating new wars, often in the aftermath of old ones. But in 1914–18, and once again in 1939–45, almost the entire world, literally, was to be plunged into global conflict, the likes of which had never been seen in the history of the world.

CHAPTER 5
THE WORLD WARS

What we today refer to as World War I (1914–18) and World War II (1939–45) were, arguably, the most significant military events in history. At their worst, they plunged most of the planet into 'total war', transforming or consuming millions of lives and scorching entire nations.

Compared to the scale of what was to follow, World War I was triggered by a relatively minor act of violence. On 28 June 1914, a young Bosnian Serb nationalist, Gavrilo Princip, fired two pistol shots into the royal car carrying the Austro-Hungarian archduke Franz Ferdinand and his wife – both of whom subsequently died from their injuries. This event, part of a Balkan resistance to the rule of the Austro-Hungarian Empire, triggered a snowballing sequence of political outcomes that led to a world in flames. The great empires of Europe – British, French, German, Austro-Hungarian, Russian and Italian – already highly militarized and on a war footing, collapsed into outright war as enmities and alliances came into play. Austria-Hungary declared war on Serbia on 28 July 1914; Russia, a Serbian protector, mobilized, resulting in Germany (an Austro-Hungarian ally) declaring war on Russia on 1 August. The French Republic, in sympathy with Russia and Serbia, then entered war against Germany on 3 August. The British Empire joined the conflict the next day – the day on which Germany turned a shouting war into a shooting war by invading Belgium –

drawn in by its alliance with France and a commitment to protect Belgium's neutrality.

WORLD WAR I

With grim momentum, the widening conflict sucked in combatants, turning a European war into a world war. Japan declared war on Germany and Austria-Hungary on 23 and 25 August 1914 respectively. In October, the Bulgarians allied themselves with the Germans, and in November, the Turkish Ottoman Empire did likewise. Together, Germany, Austria-Hungary, Bulgaria and the Ottoman Empire would be known as the Central Powers, opposing the Entente Powers of Britain, France, Russia, Japan and, from April 1915, the Kingdom of Italy. Once dozens of other nations had declared their allegiances, including the USA for the Allies in 1917, there were few corners of the world untouched by war.

The Western Front

Germany began its land campaign in Western Europe on 4 August 1914, with the invasion of Belgium and Luxembourg. The plan was to bypass the French fortifications on the Franco-German border, swing south to take Paris, knock France out of the war, then redeploy rapidly east to counter the Russian threat – above all, Germany wanted to avoid the divided energies of a two-front war.

It was not to be. The French Army and the British Expeditionary Force (BEF) together managed to blunt the German offensive within a month. Paris was saved, but there followed the 'race to the sea', the opposing sides advancing quickly to the north-west in the attempt to outflank the other. By the time the combatants reached the North Sea they had, behind them, established an unbroken chain of trench defences stretching from coastal Flanders to the Swiss frontier. It was along this bloody and battered earthen line

 Troops of the British Expeditionary Force (BEF) in Belgium in 1914. They have stacked their .303in Short Magazine Lee-Enfield (SMLE) rifles, a weapon that initially stunned the Germans with its rapidity of fire.

that the battles of the Western Front would be fought, with little meaningful change, for the next three years.

Between the end of 1914 and the spring of 1917, the strategic efforts on the Western Front followed a soul-destroying rhythm. One side would make an attempt to break through the enemy's front, followed by weeks or months of exhausting and costly fighting, at which point the offensive would burn itself out, having gained little significant advance. The main German effort came in February 1916, when the Germans assaulted the French fortified city of Verdun, intending to draw the French into a decisive battle of attrition. Attrition was certainly achieved. Verdun became one of the most destructive battles in human history, killing approximately 435,000 Germans and 540,000 French, but it achieved little in terms of advancing German war goals.

Yet aside from Verdun, the Germans mainly took a defensive posture in the years 1914–17. The Allies, by contrast, launched major offensives with dogged regularity. Many of these campaigns have become sombre landmarks in military history. For example, the Battle of the Somme, launched on 1 July 1916, ran until 18 November, and cost *c.*600,000 Allied casualties (including *c.*420,000 British) for Allied penetrations of just 10 km (6 miles). In early 1917, the Germans simply retreated back to their highly defendable 'Siegfried Line', leaving the stalemate on the Western Front largely intact.

Trench Warfare

The armies on the Western Front faced each other across the area of 'no-man's land' that separated the frontline trenches, the distances between them often measured in tens or hundreds of yards. The trench networks became works of some sophistication, typically featuring parallel lines of frontline, support and reserve trenches facing the enemy, all linked longitudinally with communications trenches to allow the movement of supplies and the rotation of frontline units. The trenches were enhanced with duckboard flooring, dugouts (the Germans made particularly deep and robust concrete underground emplacements), and even electrical lighting, but they were still horribly insanitary places in which to live and fight, especially during wet or wintry months. Soldiers found themselves knee-deep in mud and other horrors; the problems of retrieving bodies from the trench landscape often meant that the living and the dead existed side by side; vermin proliferated; shellfire was erratic but a constant threat. Yet trenches were highly defendable. Tight-packed spirals of barbed wire in front of the trenches slowed attackers to a crawl, exposing them to scythes of machine-gun, rifle, mortar and artillery fire, which cut down men in their thousands. The only way to break a trench was to get into it physically and wrest it from the hands of the enemy. It was to this endeavour that the combatants on the Western Front applied all their desperation and ingenuity.

Popular history has commonly presented the fighting on the Western Front as unfeeling and jingoistic bloodletting, wasting millions of lives for mere kilometres of blasted ground. Such a viewpoint has some ingredients of truth, but largely crumbles during closer analysis. The battle for the Western Front was fought in a series of uncompromising conditions. An endless, unbroken frontline meant that there was no flank to be turned, and reduced opportunity for sophisticated manoeuvres; all the attackers could essentially do was pound the enemy defences with artillery, then throw themselves at the trenches head on, straight into the enemy firepower, albeit with some later innovations (see below). Battlefield communications were still limited (runners, dispatch riders, fixed-line field telephones and very early wireless communications); what appear to us as unimaginative tactics were often the result of trying to achieve some degree of unit coordination across expansive fronts.

Furthermore, World War I saw the perfection of 'industrial' methods and instruments of killing. Artillery was the defining weapon, in terms of quantity, power and volume of fire. During the week-long Allied preparatory bombardment before the Somme offensive, for example, British and French artillery pieces unleashed 1.7 million shells into the opposing lines (although 30 per cent of the munitions actually did not explode). Artillery fire-control became increasingly sophisticated, the storms of shells fired precisely with the times and movements of attacking infantry.

There were other devices that added to the extreme body counts. Brutally reliable machine guns like the British Vickers and the German MG08, could put down streams of high-velocity rounds hour after hour, scything down ranks of infantry. Bolt-action rifles were now fast-firing and accurate, and the infantry was also heavily armed with light machine guns and hand grenades. Poison gas of various types, first used in earnest on the Western Front on 22 April 1915 north of Ypres, became an especially horrifying and common area weapon, its effects ranging from blistered skin to blindness and asphyxiation, inflicting 1.3 million casualties by war's end.

War, with all its logical necessity, nevertheless brought innovations as each side tried to claim the advantage, particularly in 1917 and 1918. Infantry, artillery and emerging air power became increasingly well coordinated. Infantry also gained the support of primitive tanks, first used by the British at the Battle of Flers-Courcelette (part of the Battle of the Somme) on 15 September 1916. The early tanks were lumbering, unreliable and vulnerable

 The Vickers was the standard British heavy machine gun. It could, thanks to its water-cooled barrel and with an occasional barrel change and sensible fire control, maintain sustained fire for hours.

beasts, but they did carry battlefield impact, particularly for their ability to grind through barbed wire and deliver direct fire on to enemy positions. The British and French launched some 378 tanks, along with extensive air support, coordinated artillery and improved infantry infiltration tactics, at the Battle of Cambrai on 20 November–7 December 1917, offering a new model for offensive strategy.

The grinding years of stalemate on the Western Front finally came to an end in 1918, by which time Russia had dropped out of the war, convulsed by the Revolution of 1917, and the USA had joined the Allied cause. The USA brought fresh manpower and powerful industrial output, both much needed in the coming months.

On 21 March 1918, a re-energized German military launched its 'Spring Offensive' with three full armies, in an attempt to shatter and shove back the Allied frontline. Backed by 6,437 artillery pieces, the Germans fought using innovative 'Stormtrooper' tactics, applying infantry manoeuvre and firepower to overwhelm the Allied defences. The results were, at first, astonishing, and appeared to be tipping the balance of the war. By late March, the Germans had advanced 80 km (50 miles) at the deepest point of penetration, and they kept the pressure up with repeated offensives throughout the spring and into the summer months. Yet progressively, the offensive was burning itself out, costings hundreds of thousands of lives and stretching supply lines. By this point, 10,000 US troops were arriving in-theatre every day, with 650,000 in France by May. Gradually, the Allies put the brakes on the German advance and then surged forwards themselves, not only reversing all the German gains but also pushing on towards the German homeland. By September, Germany's allies were beginning to abandon the war, suing for peace. By winter, Germany saw the futility of ongoing resistance. On 11 November, the Armistice was declared.

The Eastern Front

In contrast to much of the fighting on the Western Front, at least between 1914 and 1917, the war on the Eastern Front was characterized by movement and momentum. Russia entered the war with an impressive on-paper strength, with 5.97 million troops (standing and reserve forces) in August 1914 – larger than any other land army. But the numbers papered over the cracks. The Russian Army was often badly led and poorly equipped, and suffered accordingly. When the Russians launched their first offensive, into East Prussia, in August 1914 it took gut-punch defeats at the Battle of Tannenberg (26–30 August), at which nearly the entire Russian Second Army was destroyed, and at the First Battle of the Masurian Lakes (7–14 September). All told, the Russians may have suffered in the region of 1 million casualties in 1914 alone.

Austro-Hungarian and German forces were now on the offensive in early 1915, fighting primarily in the Carpathians, a winter campaign that inflicted attrition on both sides. Yet Russian disasters seemed to be stacking up. The Second Battle of the Masurian Lakes (7–22 February 1915) nearly wiped out the Russian Tenth Army, then the Gorlice–Tarnów Offensive (2 May–22 June) put the Russians into retreat.

Only in 1916 did Russia finally begin to reverse some of its losses. Its celebrated figure was General Alexei Brusilov, commander of the South-West Front. On 4 June, he launched the 'Brusilov Offensive', a vast pushback against the Central Powers in what is today western Ukraine. Brusilov managed to launch an offensive with 40 infantry and 15 cavalry divisions with relative surprise, keeping preparatory bombardments short and moving troops up covertly in trenches. He also applied 'fire-and-manoeuvre' infantry tactics, steering away from the crude and costly human-wave assaults used previously. The Brusilov Offensive was certainly a triumph, making major advances into Poland and Galicia, and inflicted devastating losses on the Austro-Hungarian army. Yet by the time the offensive had come to an end in September 1916, the Russians had themselves taken daunting casualties – estimates range from 500,000 to 1 million. Furthermore, the following year brought the convulsions of the Russian Revolution, which resulted in the abdication of Tsar Nicholas II and precipitated a Russian Civil War. Initially, the new revolutionary government under Alexander Kerensky had attempted to keep Russia in the fight against Germany, but increasing German offensive confidence and internal chaos led the later Bolshevik government under Vladimir Lenin to negotiate an armistice on 15 December 1917, taking Russia out of the war and freeing the Central Powers forces on the Eastern Front for service elsewhere.

Other Theatres

Although World War I did not quite reach the international scale of World War II, it was still a global conflict, not least if we include the seas as a battleground. Italy, for example, was drawn into hostilities on 23 May 1915, when it declared war on Austria-Hungary. Much of the fighting between Italy and the Austro-Hungarian Army was conducted on the northern Isonzo Front, a terrain characterized as much by its environmental as its military challenges. Thought scorching summers and sub-zero winters, the two sides slugged it out over broad valleys and craggy, high-altitude mountains, the troops in the latter often living a troglodyte existence in caves and stone-built bunkers, in thin air and deep snow.

In total, the Italians would launch nine offensives along the Isonzo Front in 1915 and 1916, with little strategic result apart from tens of thousands dead, on both sides. In 1917, the exhausted Austro-Hungarians appealed for, and received, direct military assistance from the Germans, who released six divisions from the Eastern Front. The Central Powers' offensive at Caporetto (today in north-western Slovenia) on 24 October saw the Germans apply gas, Stormtroopers and infiltration tactics with signal success, the attack breaking the integrity of Italian defences on the Isonzo and pushing back the Italian Second Army some 241km (150 miles) before the onslaught was arrested. Eventually, the Italian Front settled back into entrenched attrition, but in 1918 it was the Italians' turn to receive foreign support, in the form of British, French and American reinforcements. Thus strengthened, the Allies turned back an Austro-Hungarian offensive in June 1918 on the Piave River, then on 24 October launched a powerful offensive of their own at Vittorio Veneto. The action lasted until 4 November, during which time the Austro-Hungarians emphatically collapsed, taking more than half a million casualties (including 448,000 POWs) and losing an astonishing 5,000 artillery pieces. An Austrian–Italian armistice was then quickly signed, bringing Italy victory, albeit at the cost of 450,000–650,000 of its young men, over the four years of war.

For Britain, one of its biggest – and also its most controversial and costly – deployments was to the Dardanelles, the strait between European and Asiatic Turkey that connects the Aegean Sea with the Sea of Marmara. In early 1915, following a Russian appeal for help, the British and French decided to reclaim the Dardanelles from the Ottomans. In an operation developed and approved by Winston Churchill, then First Lord of the Admiralty, the initial effort was limited to naval shelling of Turkish coastal forts. Then, on 25 April, the first of nearly half a million men were landed, under Turkish fire, in what became the nearly 11-month 'Battle of Gallipoli'. It was a disaster. Instead of occupying the straits, the Allied troops found themselves trapped in narrow coastal beachheads, constantly hit by shellfire. Offensive actions invariably resulted in heavy loss of life, as the Allied troops battered themselves against well-emplaced Turkish positions. Having failed in all their primary objectives in the Dardanelles, the Allies withdrew between 23 November 1915 and 9 January 1916. Given Winston Churchill's subsequent rise to greatness, he was lucky that his political career did not end here.

There were many other places in which battles and campaigns were fought, which can only be mentioned in passing. They include the Caucasus, Persia, the Balkans and Mesopotamia. Two of the most strategically significant were the British campaign in Palestine and audacious German operations in German East Africa. The former was primarily fought in 1917 and 1918, during which time the British pushed out from their base in the Suez Canal Zone, cleared the Sinai Peninsula, fought three major engagements at Gaza, and occupied Jerusalem. The great British leader of this campaign was General Edmund Allenby, who went on to inflict a prodigious defeat on the Ottoman Turks at Meggido on 19–21 September 1918, helping to bring about an Ottoman capitulation the following month. On the opposing side, another inspirational leader was the German lieutenant-colonel Paul von Lettow-Vorbeck, commander in German East Africa and known to history as the 'Lion of Africa'. Leading a force of just 14,000 troops, the majority indigenous Africans, von Lettow-Vorbeck conducted a guerrilla-style campaign of such brilliance that he tied down an Allied force of 300,000 men, which was unable to defeat the wily Germans. Only the Armistice brought his resistance to an end.

Naval War

The war at sea during World War I was every bit as strategically significant as the war on land. Maritime transportation was, for most of the combatants but especially Britain, centrally important, not only for supplying the logistics of war but also for keeping civilian populations in reasonable material comfort. During the pre-war years, a naval arms race had led to the major powers – especially Britain, Germany, France and the USA – to develop Herculean fleets of capital big-gun battleships, including the most powerful 'dreadnought' types. Between 1906 and 1914, for example, Britain had commissioned 32 new capital warships, and Germany 23.

At the outbreak of hostilities, the world braced itself for major naval gun battles across the planet's contested seas and oceans, especially between the British Grand Fleet and the German High Seas Fleet. Ultimately, however, big-gun surface ships did not quite exert the influence one might have expected. There were certainly some isolated major engagements, such as the Battle of Coronel (1 November 1914), the Battle of the Falkland Islands (8 December 1914) and the Battle of Dogger Bank (24 January 1915), but for most of the time, the battleships were used in coastal bombardment or blockade roles. Then, from 31 May to 1 June 1916, in the North Sea off the coast of Denmark, came that epic meeting of the British

 The British battleship HMS Dreadnought, *which with its all-big-gun design changed the face of naval warfare and, on its commissioning in 1906, precipitated an international naval arms race.*

and German main fleets: the Battle of Jutland, a two-day running fight that cost the British 14 major ships lost to the Germans' 11. While the battle cannot be classed as a tactical victory for the British, it nevertheless demonstrated that the German Navy could not inflict defeat upon the larger Royal Navy without taking its own catastrophic surface losses. Thus the naval blockade Britain had been imposing upon Germany would remain in place.

In truth, the most significant arena of naval warfare in World War I lay not with capital ships, bristling with gunpower and openly declared power, but with submarines, coursing silently beneath the surface. In this arena, Germany led the way, with a growing fleet of U-boats. On 22 September 1914, one of these boats – *U-9*, captained by Lieutenant Commander Otto Weddigen – demonstrated the revolution these small craft offered by, in a single engagement, sinking three British armoured cruisers in the southern North Sea.

U-boats thereafter became one of the greatest threats to the Allied navies. Furthermore, in February 1915 Germany began sinking, without warning, merchant ships in British waters, a campaign that threatened to starve Britain, which relied heavily on maritime imports. The campaign also resulted in the sinking of the luxury passenger liner *Lusitania* on 7 May 1915, a German blunder that contributed towards the US entry into the war. Nevertheless, following a period of restraint between mid-1915 and early 1917, Germany unleashed unrestricted submarine warfare on incoming and outgoing UK merchant shipping until the end of the war. Only the Allied introduction of the convoy system, which statistically reduced the chances of U-boats spotting a target, and the Armistice saved Britain from an uncertain fate. The power of the U-boat would be experience, to an even greater degree, in the following world war.

CHAPTER 5

Air War

The final arena of World War I was in the air. Given that powered, controlled flight was only 12 years old by the time World War I began, it was scarcely conceivable that these fragile wire-and-fabric multi-wing aircraft could have been repurposed for war. At first, in fact, aircraft were mainly used for reconnaissance and artillery spotting, but soon they acquired basic weapons – crew-held firearms, small bombs, and darts – for destroying enemy observation balloons. Then aircraft crews began to fight one another, which led inexorably to the birth of pure fighter aircraft in 1915. These were equipped with machine guns that eventually fired directly through the propeller arc, enabling line-of-sight targeting

 The British Sopwith Camel was one of the best aerial fighter aircraft of World War I. It had excellent manoeuvrability and was armed with twin synchronized .303in Vickers machine guns.

by the pilot, which in turn meant the fighter aircraft could lock in 'dogfights' of aerial skill and violence. For those men who flew these missions, life was perilously short, measured in mere weeks, but a rare few achieved 'ace' status, notable examples including Britain's Edward 'Mick' Mannock (61 victories) and Germany's Manfred von Richthofen – aka the 'Red Baron' – with 80 victories. Fighter aircraft also came to be used in the ground-attack role in support of infantry manoeuvres, strafing enemy positions or dropping light bombs.

World War I also saw the crude birth of strategic bombing, both by German Zeppelin airships and fixed-wing aircraft. London was hit by both, a Zeppelin raid on 31 May 1915 killing 26 people and wounding 60, while an attack by Gotha bombers on 13 June 1917 left 158 dead and 425 wounded. Although airship bombers quickly became obsolete, here were premonitions of the future of air war.

World War I was a catastrophic event by any reckoning. The extraordinary four years of bloodletting left about 20 million dead and a slightly greater number of wounded. World society and politics was left shattered, not least by stripping out deep seams of national male youth. But what some regarded as the 'war to end all wars' was, in reality, the seed of an even greater world war, one that would engulf the world just 20 years later.

WORLD WAR II

The causes of World War II have greater breadth and complexity than can be studied here. Suffice to say that in Germany, the deep political, economic and social scars left by the German defeat in World War I provided the ideal conditions for the rise of a new form of German nationalism, expressed through the vicious ideological worldview of Adolf Hitler and his National Socialist German

✦ *A defining achievement of Adolf Hitler was to build a highly organized and militaristic Nazi 'brand' – including philosophy, uniforms and salutes – to which millions of disaffected Germans flocked in the 1930s.*

Workers' Party, or Nazi Party. Through a mixture of street brutality and democratic process, Hitler became the German Chancellor in 1933, going on to engineer dictatorial powers that made him the unchallenged leader of Germany; there could be no alternative voices to challenge him.

In addition to, albeit in appearance, bringing Germany out of economic depression, Hitler also put the country back on the road to militarization, in 1935 openly rejecting the armament and military manpower restrictions imposed on Germany by the Versailles Treaty in 1919. Hitler's power grew without serious challenge from the international community, even when Hitler remilitarized the Rhineland in March 1936 (forbidden by Allied treaties), annexed Austria and the Sudetenland in 1938, then conducted a bloodless annexation of the Czech parts of Czechoslovakia in March 1939. Hitler's overarching goals were *Lebensraum* ('living space') for the German people, vengeance for the defeat in World War I (during which he served bravely in the trenches) and the racial 'purity' of the German people, through the removal of the Jews and other peoples he considered racially inferior.

Poland and Western Europe

On 1 September 1939, Hitler's *Wehrmacht* (armed forces) launched the opening campaign of what would is arguably the most cataclysmic and destructive event in human history, World War II, with the invasion of Poland. Some 1.2 million men and major armoured forces crossed the German–Polish border in the first demonstration of *Blitzkrieg* (lightning war). (Note that the term is more of an historical one, rather than a label the Wehrmacht used at the time.) The professionalism and power of the revitalized German forces was proven without question. Polish forces resisted with heroic determination, at times far harder than Hitler had predicted (in one three-day battle, the Poles destroyed an entire

German infantry division), and Blitzkrieg tactics often did not go as persuasively as they had in training. Nevertheless, by 27 September the final resistance in Warsaw collapsed, and Poland entered five years of the cruellest occupation.

Blitzkrieg

The *Blitzkrieg* strategy was centred upon Panzer (armoured) divisions and mechanized infantry, which used their mobility and speed to punch through weak points (*Schwerpunkt* – 'centres of gravity') in the enemy lines and make deep penetrations, throwing enemy communications and responses into disarray. Gone were the days of broad frontal assaults – indeed, heavily defended positions were largely bypassed and avoided – and in came speed and manoeuvre as the guiding principles. The power of the armoured strike and the follow-up infantry assault was enhanced by close air support (CAS) from Luftwaffe (German Air Force) strike aircraft, such as the Junkers Ju 87 dive-bomber, which provided a form of aerial artillery. The Panzer divisions also included their own divisional infantry, engineer, anti-aircraft, anti-tank, artillery and engineer units, so could fight unliterally. The aim was to dictate a tempo of operations that the enemy simply could not match, leaving him vulnerable to pursuit, encirclement and disintegration.

On 3 September, British Prime Minister Neville Chamberlain broadcast Britain's declaration of war on Germany. France did likewise, the invasion of Poland now widening into a European conflict. In the West, however, relatively little would happen between October 1939 and April 1940, leading some in Britain to declare it the 'Phoney War'. Not so in the east, where German-allied

A Polish boy sits traumatised in the rubble of his wrecked home in Warsaw, after the German Luftwaffe reduced about 50 per cent of the city to ruins during the bombing raids of September 1939.

Soviet forces invaded Finland on 30 November 1939, beginning the three-month 'Winter War' that eventually resulted in a victory for Stalin, but at huge cost against stubborn Finnish defenders. Hitler in particular took note of the Red Army's struggles, sensing opportunity in their weakness.

Hitler knew that, with Britain and France now declared as combatants, the direction of the war would turn west. On 9 April, the Wehrmacht unleashed an invasion of Norway and Denmark, mindful that controlling Scandinavia was critical to ensuring the safe supply of iron ore shipments from Sweden. Norway was a tough nut to crack, and one that saw British, French and German troops in combat for the first time. Yet again, the Germans brought innovation to the table, not least in their first use of paratroopers to capture key airfields, bridges and positions; the application of airborne troops would be of increasing significance as the war went on.

The last Allied foothold in Norway was abandoned on 8 June, by which time the principal German campaign in the West was underway. In a campaign of genuine brilliance, German forces swept into the Netherlands and Belgium on 10 May 1940, overwhelming both quickly. Again, the airborne troops appeared; elite German paratroopers, landing in gliders, seized the Belgian frontier fortress of Eben-Emael, despite being outnumbered by more than two to one. On 13 May, German Panzer forces then attacked into France, unexpectedly emerging from the supposedly impassable Ardennes forest and bypassing the Maginot Line defences. From then on, both the French Army and the British Expeditionary Force (BEF) were outmanoeuvred and outfought. The BEF were pushed back to the coast, from where 338,000 men (including about one-third French soldiers) were evacuated to Britain by 4 June in a miraculous exercise in extraction. Paris fell on 14 June and an armistice was signed on the 22nd.

Britain Fights On

Following the conquest of France, it appeared to all in Britain that they would be next. Indeed, Hitler's plan for the invasion of the UK, Operation *Sealion*, was intended for 1940. The big obstacles to the success of that invasion, which relied on a cross-Channel assault, were the strength of Britain's Royal Navy and the resistance of the Royal Air Force (RAF). To obviate the latter, between 8 August and 30 October 1940, the Luftwaffe engaged the RAF in the 'Battle of Britain', three months of intensive, twisting aerial combat, mostly conducted over south-east England. It was a critical campaign that rested, for Britain, on the shoulders of 'The Few', as Winston Churchill (Prime Minister from 10 May 1940) called them. During these three punishing months, Britain's Spitfire and Hurricane pilots held out, downing 1,733 German aircraft for 915 of their own losses.

By the time the Battle of Britain had ended, Hitler had called off *Sealion*, not least because he was now looking east towards an invasion of the Soviet Union. In September 1940, however, the Luftwaffe switched to the night-bombing of Britain's cities – the Blitz. This was at its most intensive until May 1941, but returned sporadically until 1944, the threats also evolving to include the V-1 flying bomb and the V-2 ballistic missile, both innovations that augured Cold War technologies. The threat and reality of German bombing had a profound effect on British life: millions of children experienced evacuation from urban areas; 2 million people were rendered homeless; c.60,000 civilians were killed. Yet ultimately, it was Germany, and also its ally Japan, who would suffer the greatest hammer blows of strategic bombing in the war.

North Africa and the Balkans

Until the USA joined the war in December 1941, Britain largely fought on alone, albeit with American logistical assistance and also with the active support of Commonwealth forces, especially Australia, New Zealand, Canada, South Africa and India. The major British theatre for land operations was North Africa and the Balkans. Italy had entered the war as a German ally in June 1940, and on 13 September 1940, Italian forces in Libya made an advance into British-held Egypt, presenting a potential threat to the British-controlled Suez Canal. The British commander in the region, General Archibald Wavell, responded with a counter-offensive the following December and the Italians were routed and pushed back 800 km (500 miles), with tens of thousands of Italians captured.

Strategic Bombing

Strategic bombing refers to the deliberate policy of sustained air attacks on infrastructural, industrial and civilian housing, with the intention of breaking the enemy's will and ability to sustain the war. Such bombing was used with a certain moral reticence in 1939 and 1940, with exceptions such as the German bombing of Warsaw and Rotterdam. The greatest strategic bombing efforts, however, were conducted by the British and the Americans between 1942 and 1945. In Britain, the area bombing directive of 14 February 1942 allowed British four-engine heavy bombers – principally the British Lancaster – to strike German urban targets in mass raids, operations that the United States Army Air Force (USAAF) joined with its US B-17 Flying Fortresses and B-24 Liberators in March 1943, the British bombing by night, the Americans by day. The strikes subsequently inflicted on Germany were profound, with most major cities virtually wiped off the map by April 1945; a single infamous raid on Dresden on 13–15 February 1945 alone killed at least 25,000 people.

On the other side of the world, the USAAF XXI Bomber
Command hit Japanese cities relentlessly with firebomb attacks
from November 1944 until war's end. Hundreds of thousands
died, including some 100,000 in a single raid on Tokyo on 9–10
March 1945. Strategic bombing remains controversial to this day,
and its results are open to debate. It should be noted that neither
Germany nor Japan retaliated with similar strategies, having
neither the aircraft nor the capacity to prosecute such campaigns.

On 6 April 1941, Germany invaded Yugoslavia. The country
was forced into surrender by 17 April, but not peaceful occupation
– the subsequent internecine partisan war would cost the country
more than a million lives. Also on 6 April, the Germans invaded
Greece, actually on something of a rescue mission to bolster the
Italian forces who had been fighting with signal lack of success in
Greece since October 1940. Here, the operation was far tougher,
and it would take the entire month to clear the country of Greek
and British resistance. But Germany eventually added Greece to
its list of conquests. The next objective was the island of Crete,
base to 30,000 British and Commonwealth troops, which was
attacked on 20 May 1941 in Operation *Mercury*. This action
was one of the most striking of the war, in that it was conducted
entirely by airborne assault – German troops were deployed by
parachute, gliders and Ju 52 transport aircraft, 22,750 men in total.
In extraordinary scenes, parachute canopies blackened the blue
Aegean skies. However, thousands of the German airborne soldiers
died on the first day alone, demonstrating how vulnerable these
troops could be during their slow, floating deployment. Eventually,
the sheer professionalism and fighting abilities of the paratroopers
won through, and by 31 May the island was in German hands. The

British forces advance with fixed bayonets through the Western Desert during the Battle of El Alamein in 1942, the battle that began the eventual German defeat in North Africa.

cost – 7,000 paratroopers dead – though, meant Hitler thereafter largely confined the paratroopers to the status of elite foot infantry.

Back in North Africa, in February 1941 German forces began to arrive in the theatre, headed by one of Hitler's landmark generals, General Erwin Rommel, who had been central to both the development of Germany's armoured forces and Blitzkrieg doctrine and also the victories in the West in 1940. With Rommel in charge, the advantage now passed from one side to the other, the advances and retreats see-sawing back and forth across North Africa. Rommel's advantage lay in his skills of manoeuvre and attack; the Allies in their better logistics, with command of the Mediterranean Sea. The tide truly turned against the Germans in late 1942. First, the British Eighth Army, now under control of Lieutenant-General Bernard Montgomery, launched an irresistible offensive at El Alamein on 23 October, which inflicted irrecoverable losses on the German and Italian forces and began their retreat all the way back to Tunisia. Second, on 8 November, US and British forces invaded French North Africa, trapping Rommel in an unsustainable two-front war, especially as the bulk of German forces were by now deployed to the Eastern Front (see below). Although the US forces, facing the Germans for the first time in combat, were handled roughly at first, the momentum building up against the Germans in the theatre was irresistible, and by 11 May 1943 those Germans who had not been captured had fled north into Sicily and Italy.

Sicily and Italy

The Allied decision to invade and fight for Italy and Sicily remains a matter of strategic controversy to this day. It was largely Churchill's project, the Americans wanting to invade occupied northern Europe more directly and sooner, although it quickly became clear that wouldn't be possible logistically. Churchill proposed assaulting Sicily and Italy as the 'soft underbelly' of Europe, drawing German forces away from the future battlegrounds of northern Europe while also relieving some pressure on the Soviets on the Eastern Front. Thus on 9 July 1943, the US Seventh Army and the British Eighth Army invaded Sicily in Operation *Husky*, one of the biggest amphibious invasions of all time. The fighting, though tough, saw the German forces cleared from the island by 17 August, although many of the German troops simply crossed the Straits of Messina into mainland Italy.

The subsequent campaign to clear Italy itself, contrary to the 'soft underbelly' label, was brutally hard-fought. This reality was despite the fact that the Italians negotiated an armistice with the Allies on 3 September 1943, the very day when Allied forces began landing in the south of the country. Italy was a struggle from the beginning, despite the Allies having complete superiority in sea power and airpower. The German commander in Italy, General Field Marshal Albert Kesselring, conducted brilliant defensive actions, anchored on a series of defensive lines embedded in Italy's mountainous interior and river lines. Both the Allied landings at Salerno (9 September 1943) and Anzio (22 January 1944) struggled to gain and exploit their footholds, and the fighting at Monte Cassino between 12 February and May 18 1944 was harrowing in the extreme, an eventual Allied victory that cost the American Fifth Army and the British Eighth Army 55,000 casualties. Yet steadily the Allies inched up the country, taking Rome on 4 June and confining the Germans in the far north of the country, where they stayed until the German surrender in May 1945.

D-Day and Victory in the West

Although planning for the liberation of North-West Europe had begun back in 1940, it wasn't until 6 June 1944 that this objective became a reality in Operation *Overlord*. On that day, at around 0600 hrs, landing craft began depositing the first of nearly 133,000

American, British, Canadian and Commonwealth troops on to the beaches of Normandy, having been preceded by some 20,000 airborne troops who dropped into the region over the preceding hours. The landings were a potent demonstration of Allied logistical, naval and amphibious capabilities, delivered or supported by 5,333 ships, and also its ability to claim total air superiority – the 8,268 Allied aircraft operational over the landing areas quickly saw off meagre Luftwaffe opposition. Although the landings were heavily contested in places, especially at the American 'Omaha Beach' landing zone, by nightfall the Allies were securely ashore for about 3,400 killed or missing; original casualty estimates had been in the tens of thousands. From the beachhead began the advance into the interior, against trenchant German opposition that turned every street, hedgerow, town and village into a battlefield. The breakout, led by the US Third Army under General George S. Patton, began in earnest in August 1944, and by 5 August Paris had been liberated.

By September 1944, the Allies were on the German frontier, and attempted to expedite Germany's collapse through Operation *Market Garden* (17–25 September). The plan was for the First Allied Airborne Army – some 41,600 British and American paratroopers – to drop into enemy territory and seize bridgeheads over the River Rhine, holding them as the British XXX Corps advanced overland to relieve them. It was a profound failure, as heavy German resistance prevented XXX Corps from punching through, which left the British 1st Airborne Division at Arnhem isolated and nearly destroyed, losing 8,000 men.

Airborne Troops

The development of airborne forces (parachute and air-landed troops) had been pioneered in the Soviet Union, Italy and

Germany during the 1930s, with Germany taking the lead by the onset of World War II. Britain and the USA began to acquire their own airborne units in 1940, but by 1944 had established entire airborne divisions, by which time the Germans, stung by their experience on Crete (see above), had largely retracted the airborne role. Airborne troops provided a new vertical dimension to infantry tactics, meaning that soldiers could be landed directly over the mission objective area, or at least close to it, bypassing defences or difficult terrain obstacles. Paratroopers enabled a variety of potential missions: cutting enemy supply lines; seizing and holding high-value targets; reinforcing or rescuing surrounded forces; diverting enemy troops away from ground operations. Airborne troops, however, necessarily went into action 'light', with little equipment, heavy weaponry and supplies, so it was imperative that they be relieved or resupplied within days of landing.

The residual fighting energy of the Germans was also demonstrated when, on 16 December 1944, they launched a vast counter-offensive through the wintery Ardennes forest, intended to split the Allied armies and ultimately capture Antwerp. Involving 410,000 men, more than 1,400 armoured vehicles and 3,200 artillery pieces, the offensive initially made startling progress, with deep advances in some sectors and surrounding US troops in Bastogne. Yet eventually the momentum bled away under heavy losses and logistical difficulties, and the clearing of skies in January 1945 meant that Allied airpower was able to resume its savaging of German armour.

The 'Battle of the Bulge', as it is known, was Hitler's last offensive gasp in the West. The Allies thereafter pushed on into the Netherlands and Germany, linking up with the Russians on the Elbe on 25 April. Five days later, Hitler committed suicide and the German unconditional surrender followed shortly after, on 4 May, with the formal surrender on 7 May.

The U-boat War

The naval war between the Western Allies did feature some major surface engagements, notably the clashes with the battleship *Bismarck* in May 1941. The most significant element, however, was the Allied struggle against the U-boats, especially in the Atlantic Ocean. At the onset of war, the German Navy had a 57 U-boats in the fleet, but in total would produce 1,141 combat submarines between 1939 and 1945. Hunting in coordinated 'Wolf Packs', the U-boats began preying on Britain's transatlantic lifeline, and with considerable effect. In 1940, 2.4 million GRT (gross registered tonnage) of Allied ships were sunk by the U-boats, but in 1942 this annual total swelled to 6.1 million GRT, fostered by the proliferation of new merchant targets on US entry into the war. For a time, the U-boats were sinking Allied vessels faster than the Allies could replace them, and there was the danger that Britain could be starved into defeat. Yet steadily the tide turned through a mix of Allied tactical and technical innovations: improved convoy escort tactics; better shipboard and aircraft-mounted U-boat detection technologies (radar and acoustic); the introduction of very-long-range anti-submarine aircraft; improved intelligence on U-boat movements through the breaking of the Enigma military code. Eventually, the tide turned so much that being a member of a U-boat crew was ultimately the most dangerous job in the German military – 821 U-boats would be sunk by the end of the war.

The Eastern Front

Of all the fateful decisions made by Hitler during the war, it was his invasion of the Soviet Union on 22 June 1941 that, with hindsight, sealed Germany's fate. At first, this was far from evident, as the invasion – by three massive army groups (North, Centre and South) – comprising 3 million men was initially supremely victorious. The Red Army, massive in terms of manpower but weak in command, control and training, collapsed precipitously on all fronts. The Soviets took c.4 million casualties by December, by which time the Germans had reached Leningrad in the north, the outskirts of Moscow in the centre, and beyond Kharkov in the Ukraine. Only the onset of the paralyzing Soviet winter and the redeployment of troops from Siberia saved the Russian capital from falling.

When spring arrived in 1942, the Germans resumed their offensive, this time concentrating their efforts on a southern drive into the Caucasus, which held the bulk of the Soviet Union's oil production plants. This advance, which for a time seemed to repeat the German glories of 1941, led to the epic battle at Stalingrad on the Volga, a city for which both sides fought without restraint or mercy from August 1942 to February 1943. The battle, costing more than a million lives, ended with the encirclement and destruction of the German Sixth Army, an unprecedented defeat for Germany and a galvanizing victory for the Soviets.

The Red Army now began to gather offensive momentum, despite numerous setbacks. On 5 July 1943, the two sides locked horns in the Battle of Kursk, the largest tank battle in history, involving more than 8,000 armoured vehicles. As this steely engagement indicates, armour had become, alongside artillery, the chief tool in land warfare, deployed in huge numbers and with ever-increasing firepower, mobility and armoured protection. The Germans produced a wide spectrum of tank types, the most formidable being the PzKpfw IV, the PzKpfw VI Tiger and the

PzKpfw V Panther, all of which inflicted a disproportionate toll on Allied armies. The Soviets opted to produce more than 84,000 of the basic but excellent T-34 and T-34-85 tanks, characterized by their speed, cross-country mobility, effective armour and suitability for mass production. This distinction between German technical specialization vs Allied mass production can be seen in many areas of World War II technology. Ultimately, mass production won out.

The Battle of Kursk was, in the final analysis, a Soviet victory. What it also began was the steady retreat of the German forces back to Germany itself, the shattered divisions suffering terribly on the way. By 12 January 1945, the Red Army was across the German border, and on 16 April the assault on Berlin began. Although resistance was futile, German troops in Berlin fought with ferocity, inflicting more than 300,000 casualties on the Soviets in these last acts of the European War. Hitler's suicide shaved a few days off the inevitable, and eventually the ruined capital of Hitler's 'Thousand Year Reich' descended into the silence of surrender.

The war on the Eastern Front was Hitler's greatest error, alongside declaring war on the USA, a country that through its incomparable industrial energy became the logistical and armament powerhouse of the war. Taken together, the Allies produced volumes of men and materiel Germany (and Japan) simply couldn't match. But turning back to the Eastern Front, here was a conflict totally unsuited to Germany's war machine. The endless distances stretched and drained supply chains, and soaked up and dispersed offensive actions; the freezing sub-zero winters reduced armoured vehicles to frozen blocks of metal; the relentless battles cost equally endless casualties – the Germans suffered 5.1 million dead on the Eastern Front, whereas the Western Front cost them *c*.600,000 dead. And the Soviets? Total losses, civilian and military, number somewhere around 25 million. Truly did the Soviets pay for the Allied victory in blood.

War in the Pacific

While the Pacific War certainly connects to the fighting further west, it was in many ways largely independent of the European war, at least until the final weeks of conflict. Political and economic tensions between an imperial Japan and the West, particularly the USA, had been squeezing ever tighter during the 1920s and 1930s, resulting in the USA imposing an oil embargo in July 1941. By this point, Japan was already a member of the Tripartite Pact with Germany and Italy, and nationalistic elements within the government were looking to expand Japanese territories through military means into South-east Asia and the Pacific, thereby overcoming the island nation's acute lack of indigenous raw materials. The Japanese, however, knew that first they had to neuter US naval power.

On 7 December 1941, therefore, 360 Japanese carrier aircraft attacked the US Pacific Fleet base at Pearl Harbor. Although they inflicted great damage, sinking or seriously damaging 14 vessels and killing 3,300 Americans, the crucial US carriers were actually away from port at this time. In reality, Japan had simply awakened a sleeping giant.

Carrier Warfare

Early aircraft carriers had been developed in the later years of World War I, but it was during the 1920s and 1930s that the ship type became a major component of navies, particularly those of the Americans, Japanese and British. Aircraft carriers varied significantly in size and air strength, from small escort carriers transporting about 30 aircraft to large fleet carriers

---

✦ *Japanese naval strike aircraft swarm over the US Navy's Pacific Fleet base in Hawaii during the attack of 7 December 1941. The attack was launched by six aircraft carriers and 420 aircraft.*

with nearly 100 aircraft on board. But the presence of carriers literally transformed naval warfare. They were the most powerful ships on the seas, capable of deploying fighters, dive-bombers and torpedo aircraft out to a range of many hundreds of kilometres. Even the greatest battleships were terribly vulnerable to their swarms of aircraft – the largest battleships in history, the Japanese vessels *Musashi* and *Yamato*, were both wiped out by US carrier strikes in 1944 and 1945 respectively. In the Pacific War, the two sides locked horns in massive carrier vs carrier actions, each side recognizing that these vessels were the key to naval supremacy. The USA, however, was virtually destined to prevail, through its awesome carrier manufacturing rates – it produced 141 carriers between 1939 and 1945, as opposed to 16 by Japan – and its far higher standards of air crew and aircraft.

Expansion and Retreat

At the same moment as Pearl Harbor was hit, the Japanese launched a land invasion that swept throughout the Pacific and South-east Asia, overrunning many European colonies and US territories in the process. The extent of the advance was every bit as impressive as that achieved by Germany in the West. Territories fell in rapid order during the remainder of 1941 and the first half of 1942 – Thailand, Malaya, Singapore, Hong Kong, Burma, the Philippines, Borneo, the Dutch East Indies, much of New Guinea, New Britain, numerous islands throughout the Pacific, including the Marianas, Gilberts, Solomons and Wake Island. Allied ground forces were overwhelmed by nimble and fast-moving Japanese manoeuvre warfare. The British fortress island of Singapore, for example, was lost in a week of fighting in February 1942, resulting in about

80,000 British, Indian and Australian troops going into captivity, which Winston Churchill labelled the 'worst disaster' in British military history. Steadily, the Japanese advance slowed, however, and the Allies began the fightback, especially at the hands of a vengeful USA.

The all-important war at sea tipped in US favour at the Battle of the Coral Sea (4–8 May 1942) and the Battle of Midway (4–7 June 1942), epic carrier engagements resulting in the Japanese Navy losing five of its carriers (four fleet carriers at Midway alone). In New Guinea, a Japanese offensive along the Owen Stanley mountain range in late July 1942 was gradually stopped then pushed back by Australian and US forces, and on 7 August 1942, US troops invaded the southern Solomon Islands, eventually expelling the Japanese from Guadalcanal by February 1943. The British began campaigning into occupied Burma in December 1942, although it would be 1944–5 before serious territorial gains were made.

It was from 1943 that the new Japanese Empire began to retract significantly, a process that gathered a drumbeat pace in 1944 and 1945. The US strategy divided the Pacific into two main theatres. General Douglas MacArthur took command of the South-West Pacific Area, his objectives being the liberation of New Guinea, the Solomons, the Philippines, Borneo, the Bismarck Archipelago and the Dutch East Indies. Admiral Chester Nimitz took charge of the Pacific Ocean Areas; his forces were to conduct a vast 'island-hopping' campaign across the Pacific, landing upon and clearing the numerous heavily defended islands leading across the Central Pacific to the Japanese homeland itself. Caught between these US offensives, the British and Commonwealth effort in Burma, and also Japan's war in China (which it had been fighting since 1937), Japan was now caught in a vast international compress.

The Pacific campaigns fought between November 1943 and August 1945 were characterized by exceptional brutality. Small, isolated islands, often little more than coral outcrops, became the sites of literal fights to the death for the Japanese occupiers, who invariably inflicted terrible casualties on the US troops. The battle for Tarawa (20–23 November 1943), for example, saw the deaths of 1,696 Americans and 4,690 Japanese (only 17 Japanese were captured) for a scrap of land just 4 km (2.5 miles) long and 720 m (800 yards) wide at its widest point. The major island battles of Iwo Jima (19 February–26 March 1945) and Okinawa (1 April–22 June 1945) saw apocalyptic levels of bloodshed; Okinawa alone cost the lives of *c.*20,000 US troops and *c.*110,000 Japanese. A similar experience was had by MacArthur's troops in the South-West Pacific Area; the month-long urban battle for Manila in the Philippines in February 1945 resulted in *c.*6,000 military and more than 100,000 civilian fatalities. Japanese tactics included the widespread use of suicide kamikaze aircraft to attack the US invasion fleets and equally suicidal *banzai* charges as a last-ditch infantry tactic.

But steadily the net closed around Japan, squeezed tighter by the relentless strategic bombing of Japanese cities and the enormously effective US submarine war, which sank about 200 Japanese warships and more than 1,000 merchant vessels. At its close, however, the Pacific War was not finalized by a culminating land battle, but in the deployment of two monstrous pieces of technology. On 6 August 1945, the city of Hiroshima was wiped from the map by the detonation of an atomic bomb about 580 m (1,900 ft) above the streets; some 80,000 people died in mere seconds. Nagasaki suffered the same fate on 9 August. The atomic bombs, developed under the Americans' 'Manhattan Project' since 1942, changed the face of warfare in an instant. Japan surrendered on 15 August, signing the Instrument of Surrender aboard the USS *Missouri*, anchored in Tokyo Bay, on 2 September 1945. World War II was over.

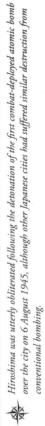

Hiroshima was utterly obliterated following the detonation of the first combat-deployed atomic bomb over the city on 6 August 1945, although other Japanese cities had suffered similar destruction from conventional bombing.

World War II was emphatically the expression of 'total war'. The notion of the 'enemy' broadened, as military might was unleashed against both military armies and civilian populations. Entire national societies were mobilized or implicated in the war effort. The final global death toll is unknown, but lies in the region of 70–85 million, if we include 19–25 million from the diseases and famines generated by the war (which we should). About three-quarters of those deaths were civilian, illustrating in dreadful fashion how total war wrapped its arms around non-combatants.

The sheer destructiveness of World War II was made possible by the combination of ever-more powerful weapon systems – especially in terms of armour, artillery, aircraft, ordnance, small arms and mines – combined with the industrial might to produce them in huge volumes and the ideological will to fight for the complete destruction or submission of the enemy. The conflict reshaped the world, geographically and politically. But although a global war was over, the next half-century would be a long way from peace.

CHAPTER 6
THE COLD WAR

The end of the World War II was welcomed with gratitude by a conflict-weary planet. For many, however, the subsequent 'Cold War' brought little but a continuation of fighting, or provided the ingredients for making new wars in the near future. From 1945 until the fall of the Soviet Union in 1991, there was scarcely a day when war of some description did not rage in multiple locations around the world.

The Cold War is a strange time in the development of warfare. The term itself refers to the period of history between 1947 and 1991, when the capitalist West, led by the superpower USA, and the communist Soviet Union and Eastern Bloc glowered at each other with divided ideologies. Nor was the communist/capitalist tension confined to first-world states of the northern hemisphere, but formed truly global fault lines, snaking through nations, regions and continents. The tension between the Soviet Union and the West became increasingly acute, teetering on several occasions on the brink of outright war.

Thankfully, given that the Cold War was a nuclear age, the two superpowers never actually came to direct blows. Yet around the world, these superpowers provided support, direct or covert, for myriad 'proxy wars', conflicts that ranged from low-level minor insurgencies to major international conventional wars. Add to this mix the conflicts caused by post-colonial nationalism, religious

By 1975, the Soviet Army had a total of 50 tank divisions. Here T-72 tanks rumble through Russian streets during a military parade, always a useful opportunity for Western observers to check out the latest Soviet hardware.

extremism and ever-multiplying movements of radical terrorism, and we can hardly say that the world was at peace in the aftermath of World War II.

NEW WAYS OF WAR

The half-century from 1945 onwards saw some critical shifts in the practice of war-making, driven both by human and political motivations and also by technological innovations. World War II ended with the USA as the world's only nuclear-armed superpower, a fact that gave it an undeniable strategic authority over the Soviet Union. Then, on 29 August 1949, the Soviet Union detonated its first atomic bomb at the Semipalatinsk Test Site in Kazakhstan, thereby re-engineering the international balance of power. A nuclear arms race ensued, measured both by the numbers of warheads on each side but also by the nature of the delivery vehicles. At first, atomic and nuclear weapons were deployed by heavy bombers, which would have to fly into enemy airspace to deliver their payload. These were monster aircraft such as the B-52 Stratofortress and the Tupolev Tu-16 (NATO reporting name: Badger), but as nuclear bombs themselves became more compact, the weapons could be delivered by smaller, faster single-seat or dual-seat jets, better able to wind through the opposing air defences.

But the most important step in nuclear weapon delivery came during the 1950s, with the development of the first intercontinental ballistic missiles (ICBMs). The world had already witnessed the lethal supersonic potential of the ballistic missile in 1944 and 1945, in the form of the German V-2 rocket. Once nuclear weapons were married with ICBMs – early examples include the Soviet R-7 and the US Atlas – and as the capabilities of the weapons increased in terms of range and destructive lethality, then the superpowers and their allies recognized that nuclear war would almost certainly result in one's own obliteration as well as that of the enemy. Thus, during the 1960s the world entered the era of 'Mutually Assured Destruction' (MAD), effectively a nuclear stalemate that, if broken, had the potential to wipe out much of the human race within hours, if not minutes.

Yet under the shadow of the nuclear threat, the Cold War was also a time of continuing revolutions in the technologies of conventional warfare. Some of these revolutions might have appeared minor, but actually had a transformative effect on post-war global security. A prime example is the invention of the AK-47 by one Mikhail Timofeyevich Kalashnikov. The AK-47 is the pioneer of the 'assault rifle' type, a practical halfway house between a submarine gun and a full-blown rifle that would come to dominate military small arms. The AK-47 was basic, endlessly robust, easy to operate and powerful, and it became the standard rifle of the Soviet armed forces in 1949. Thereafter, it was produced on an unimaginable scale – an estimated 100 million AK-type weapons (including variants and locally produced versions) today flood the world, making it the most mass-produced weapon in history. Because of its ubiquity, it fuelled entire wars.

Beyond small arms, land warfare was still governed by two forces: infantry and armour. The infantry, despite their new small arms (the West also bought into the assault rifle concept with weapons such as the US M16), still largely fought as their World War II predecessors did, but with some changes. Infantry anti-tank weapons, for example, became far more effective, with anti-tank guided weapons (ATGWs) such as the French SS.10 and the British/Australian Malkara leading the way. Command-guided to their target at first by a controller with a joystick, but much later (1990s) acquiring 'fire-and-forget' self-guiding capabilities, the ATGMs gave infantry the tools to destroy heavy armour at thousands of metres' range. Effective surface-to-air missile (SAM) systems also entered the stage, both large emplaced and vehicle-

The SM-65 Atlas was the first intercontinental ballistic missile (ICBM) to enter US military service, and was in service between 1959 and 1965. The rocket also had a successful career as a space launch vehicle.

mounted systems for long-range interceptions, and also Man-portable Air-Defense Systems (MANPADS) varieties, such as the US Redeye and Soviet 9K32 Strela-2, that could be fired from the shoulder against low-flying aircraft.

Armour was much improved during the Cold War, especially in terms of fire-control and gun stabilization (dramatically raising the possibility of a first-round hit), manoeuvrability, amphibious properties, NBC (Nuclear, Biological, Chemical) resistance and survivability. New types of wheeled and tracked armoured vehicles also entered service, such as armoured personnel carriers (APCs) like the ubiquitous US M113, and what we today call infantry fighting vehicles (IFVs), which combined the 'battle taxi' functions of an APC with turreted guns or missile firepower that could take on even main battle tanks (MBTs).

If we were to argue for the biggest change in conventional warfare, however, we might convincingly opt for airpower. The first jet aircraft emerged in World War II, with German jets such as the Me 262, but during the post-war years the speed, combat capability and raw power of these aircraft reached astonishing levels, as the old turboprops fell away almost entirely into obsolescence as combat types. To take a great Cold War example, the McDonnell Douglas F-4E Phantom had a top speed of Mach 2.3 and could carry up to 8,480 kg (18,650 lb) of ordnance in a two-seat aircraft, more than double the bombload of a World War II B-17 Flying Fortress, which had a ten-man crew and a top speed of 462 km/h (182 mph). Other landmark Cold War jets include the Soviet MiG-21, the British English Electric Lightning and the French Dassault Mirage F1. The ordnance that these aircraft carried also underwent a leap forwards, including guided air-to-air missiles (AAMs) that could track and kill enemy aircraft dozens of miles away and a growing arsenal of precision guided munitions (PGMs) – bombs that could land within a few metres of the intended target (although 'dumb'

The FIM-92 Stinger surface-to-air missile (SAM) was widely distributed by the United States to mujahideen insurgents to counter Soviet aircraft threats during the Soviet–Afghan War of 1979–89.

unguided bombs would remain the bulk of the bombs dropped in war until the 1990s).

At sea, the Cold War era saw the sun finally, emphatically, set over the age of the big-gun battleship. The aircraft carrier still reigned supreme on the surface, especially in the US Navy which, with the USS *Enterprise* (CVN-65), in service from 1961, ushered in the age of the nuclear-powered supercarrier. These immense vessels, carrying more than 90 aircraft and embodied most numerously in the *Nimitz*-class carriers, had nuclear-reactor powerplants that could drive and power the ship for two decades without refuelling, giving the warships almost limitless range. Some submarines also received nuclear powerplants, the first being USS *Nautilus* (SSN-571), launched in 1954. If anything, the marriage of nuclear power with the submarine was even more revolutionary than nuclear surface ships. It meant that the submarine could make submerged patrols of many months' duration, loitering in the backyard of the enemy unseen. At the end of the 1950s, furthermore, the first submarines capable of launching nuclear ballistic missiles from underwater entered service. Therefore, a single submarine, by the 1960s, had acquired the capability to destroy multiple cities in a coordinated strike.

Computerization and Warfare

Underpinning most of the weapon advancements outlined above were the tectonic shifts in electronic technology that occurred in the second half of the 20th century, particularly the rise of digital computerization and the progressive miniaturization of digital components. The first monolithic integrated circuit – the microchip – and the first stored-program digital computer all emerged in the 1950s, while in the subsequent decade came the first satellite navigation system and, in 1969, the Advanced Research Projects Agency Network (ARPANET), in many ways the military forerunner of the internet. While these inventions came to affect civilian life as much as military technology, they delivered a steady revolution at the heart of professional and well-funded armies. Not only did weapons acquire a precision lethality unseen in previous generations, but command-and-control and communications achieved ever-greater reach and efficiencies, enabling the secure coordination of global forces in real time across the battlespace. If anything, it was the development of communication technologies that arguably was the most important of the post-war transformations in military practice.

As we shall see as we progress into the wars and battles of this chapter, however, it was not just technology that was changing the face of war. Despite the fact that the post-war world had more than its fair share of conventional conflicts, this was also the age of guerrilla warfare, insurgency and terrorism. Although the principles of low-level warfare are nearly as old as military history themselves, after 1945 they became codified more formally as tactical routes to final victory, particularly through communist leaders such as China's Mao Zedong and Vietnam's Ho Chi Minh. The 1950s–80s were a revolutionary age, ideologically charged, and insurgency and terrorism offered means by which even the most diminutive and poorly equipped organizations could make their presence felt on the world stage. There were few nations on earth during this time that did not periodically suffer the effects of terrorism within their own borders.

CHINA AND KOREA

In China, World War II was actually something of an interruption to an existing civil war, a conflict between communists and nationalists that had been raging since 1927. With the Japanese invaders defeated, the two sides reconnected with their former struggle. The nationalist Kuomintang, led by Jiang Jieshi (Chiang Kai-shek), had some on-paper advantages: it outnumbered the communist People's Liberation Army (PLA) three to one in 1946; it had more conventional structures and weaponry; and it had the financial investment of the USA, which contributed more than $400 million to the nationalist coffers. It was a corrupt and demoralized force, however, whose behaviour quickly lost moral high ground to the communists, led by Mao Zedong. Mao, the radicalized son of a peasant farmer, brought together a force that suffered greatly on campaign but that was highly motivated, persistent and increasingly favoured by China's civilian population. Mao preached the tenets of 'revolutionary war', a gradual path to victory that worked progressively from low-level insurgency through to open battle.

Mao Zedong – Three Principles of Revolutionary Warfare

The core principles of revolutionary warfare are critical to the evolution of many post-1945 conflicts. Mao recognized that in the early stages of a revolutionary war, the revolutionary forces would usually be inferior to the state opponents in terms of size and combat capability. Therefore, his model for conducting the campaign worked on a steady and logical expansion of both military and political activity. He outlined three core stages of revolutionary warfare:

1. Organization, consolidation and preservation of base areas

During this first phase, the revolutionaries concentrate on building up their organization at grass-roots level, establishing bases and support in remote areas, recruiting, spreading propaganda and acquiring and stockpiling weaponry.

2. Terrorism/insurgency

In the next phase, the revolutionaries begin taking small, frequent bites out of the enemy, conducting assassinations, limited attacks on isolated outposts, bombings, kidnappings, sabotage and ambushes, thus demoralizing and weakening the enemy while at the same time the revolutionaries grow stronger and more militarily confident. The key element to this stage is that the revolutionaries avoid major pitched battles, adopting a hit-and-run approach.

3. Decision, or destruction of the enemy in battle

The revolutionaries, now having grown to be a well-equipped and formally organized army, moves to open conventional warfare, finally achieving victory over an enemy already weakened by years of attrition warfare.

This model of warfare would be adopted and adapted by revolutionary armies worldwide. The Chinese victories in the civil war, and those of the Viet Minh then North Vietnam between 1945 and 1975, showed that revolutionary warfare could be a war-winning formula.

In 1946–7, it was the nationalists who seemed ascendant, winning the big offensives. But the PLA's strength was ever-growing, and in September 1948–January 1949 they took a massive victory in Shandong Province; by 10 January 1949, the nationalists had lost 250,000 men in combat, and tens of thousands more through desertion to the PLA. Tianjin and Beijing fell to the communists on 15 and 22 January 1949 respectively. From April 1948 to April 1949, the PLA steadily cleared southern China of nationalist resistance, the remaining nationalist leadership fleeing to Formosa (Taiwan) on 10 December. By this time, Mao had already publicly declared victory and the establishment of the People's Republic of China (PRC), on 1 October 1949.

Between 1945 and 1950, the USA already found itself embroiled in providing material and financial support in the war against spreading global communism. In 1950, however, began a conflict that saw US troops taking a more direct combat role in this effort. On 25 June 1950, the army of North Korea – a Soviet- and Chinese-backed communist state – invaded the capitalist and US-backed South, the Republic of Korea (ROK), across the 38th parallel– the geographic border between the two ideologies laid down imperfectly after the Japanese occupiers were expelled in 1945. In response, the USA deployed troops from occupation duties in Japan to stem the tide. However, they and the ROK army were driven relentlessly back, until they occupied a small perimeter around the port of Pusan in the far south. The UN soon joined the effort with multinational forces, including troops from Britain, Australia, Canada and France, the polyglot army eventually numbering more than 16 nations.

Eventually, the communist tide was reversed, not least by a daring amphibious outflanking operation by General Douglas MacArthur (in command of the UN Army) at the port of Inchon on 15 September 1950. The UN army began a drive northwards,

The US amphibious landing at Inchon was a bold move during the Korean War by General Douglas MacArthur. Tidal variations at Inchon meant the beaches could be used only six hours in every 24 hours.

eventually pushing the North Korean Army (NKA) back into and up through North Korea itself, taking the capital Pyongyang and advancing on the Yalu on the border with China. Just when final victory seemed inevitable, there was a major escalation – a threatened China sent hundred of thousands of PLA troops across the border in November 1950, and their offensive over the next few months cancelled out most of the UN gains and pushed deep into the South. The communist advance was eventually stopped by the application of enormous amounts of UN firepower, then reversed by a UN offensive. It was a wearying to and fro. Eventually, in 1951 the war reached something of a stalemate where it originally began, on the 38th parallel. Fighting continued sporadically with varying intensity over the next two years, until an Armistice was signed on 27 July 1953. One of the first major ideological wars of the post-war world ended with little glory for either side.

SOUTH-EAST ASIA

French Indochina War

Like Korea, most of South-east Asia was occupied by the Japanese during World War II. Also like Korea, the end of the world war would unleash new forces of schism, nationalism and ideology, leading to one of the most destructive and prolonged periods of conflict in post-1945 history.

Before the Japanese occupation, what we today know as Vietnam, Laos and Cambodia were a French colony, collectively known as French Indochina. During the occupation, the French authorities remained in situ, albeit directed by the collaborationist Vichy regime in France. Anti-Japanese resistance actually came from the communist Vietnamese People's Liberation Army (VPLA), headed by Ho Chi Minh – one of the seminal revolutionary leaders of the 20th century – and his capable general Vo Nguyen Giap. When the French therefore attempted to return to rule Indochina in late 1945, the Viet Minh were quite naturally reluctant to let their country return to full colonial rule. The French thus found themselves embarking on what would be a nine-year war against the Viet Minh.

As with the Korean War, the French Indochina War attracted powerful foreign backers. The USA, eager to prevent the spread of communism wherever it found it, supported the French with increasingly impressive amounts of money and materiel. The Viet Minh was backed by the Soviet Union and, from 1949, the nearly created PRC across the northern border; having a powerful communist neighbour was a welcome assistance to Viet Minh logistics, as well as providing secure locations for Viet Minh training and basing.

True to the principles of revolutionary war, the Viet Minh fought an intense insurgency war for the first five years, mainly in the north of Indochina, which by 1950 was largely under Viet Minh control. The French armed forces struggled to pacify these areas, despite a series of brutal operations, and found that the Viet Minh were becoming progressively bolder in their tactics and ambitions. In 1951, Giap decided to move the war forwards with an all-out offensive in the Red River Delta. This was largely broken against French defensive positions, but still the war was enmired in stalemate.

In 1953, the French looked to break the impasse with a risky new strategy. In November, French paratroopers began dropping into the isolated village of Dien Bien Phu, deep in the heart of Viet Minh territory. The plan was to reinforce the position through aerial resupply (French engineers restored an existing airstrip) and the construction of a series of strongpoints, heavily supported by artillery, and draw the Viet Minh into an open battle in which they would be destroyed by superior French firepower, including its close air support. This plan made the fatal error of underestimating the opponent. Using muscle power alone, the Viet Minh hauled hundreds of artillery pieces through the jungle and emplaced them on the hills surrounding Dien Bien Phu in the valley below; in total, these guns would pour 150,000 shells into French positions over the course of the battle. With tens of thousands of Viet Minh infantry also deployed on the campaign, Dien Bien Phu soon found itself encircled and under siege.

The siege has gone down as a landmark event in modern French military history. Over a period of two months, the French defences steadily collapsed, despite imposing heavy casualties upon the Viet Minh. Progressively, all the strongpoints fell to communist infantry assaults, and the French were squeezed into an ever-narrowing stretch of land. On 7 May 1954, Dien Bien Phu fell, a genuine catastrophe for French military prestige. Of the 15,709 French troops who fought there, more than 1,700 had been killed and 11,700 had been taken prisoner, of whom 4,400 were wounded. Only 73 men managed to escape.

The defeat at Dien Bien Phu brought an end to French rule over Indochina. Laos, Cambodia and Vietnam all became independent, although the latter was temporarily divided at the 17th parallel, with a communist North Vietnam and a US-backed Republic of Vietnam (RVN) in the south, pending reunification elections. Yet instead of reunification, the region would go on to another two decades of war.

The Vietnam War

The Vietnam War was a formative event in US military history, and is still a cautionary tale for politicians and strategists. The failure of North/South reunification led to a swelling communist insurgency in the RVN, one that corrupt southern governments and a weak Army of the Republic of Vietnam (ARVN) struggled to contain. The USA, still ideologically committed to stopping the spread of global communism, channelled its customary high volumes of money and materiel into the South, and also increased the numbers of US military 'advisors', who during the first half of the 1960s slipped frequently into combat roles. Then in August 1964, a series of ill-defined attacks by North Vietnamese fast attack craft on US shipping in the Gulf of Tonkin led to the US Congress passing the Gulf of Tonkin Resolution, under which President Lyndon Johnson effectively had the power to deploy US combat troops directly into the war zone. Following further attacks by the Viet Cong (VC) – the title applied to the southern-based insurgent National Liberation Front – on US bases in 1965, Johnson ordered the deployment of the first US brigades, the beginning of a huge escalation. By the end of 1965, there would be 184,300 US troops in-country; by the end of 1968, that number would peak at 536,100.

So it was that the USA, and the full resources of its Army, Air Force, Navy and Marine Corps came to be at the frontline of the war in Vietnam, alongside the ARVN. (The ARVN role in the Vietnam War is often overshadowed by discussion of the US campaign, but it actually conducted much of the fighting during the war and had far greater troop numbers.) The allies faced two main enemies: the People's Army of Vietnam (PAVN), which were the regular armed forces of North Vietnam, increasingly infiltrating into the south along the 'Ho Chi Minh Trail' through Laos and Cambodia; and the VC insurgency, which often worked closely with the PAVN. From 1965 to 1968, the USA expressed itself through a heavy bombing campaign – Operation *Rolling Thunder* – directed against North Vietnam's infrastructure, while in South Vietnam it conducted a series of 'search-and-destroy' missions designed to find and wipe out PAVN/VC units and bases. The overall allied strategy was as vague as it was aggressive. General William Westmoreland, the head of Military Assistance Command, Vietnam (MACV), mainly focused US efforts on attrition, a mission's success judged

Flying under radar control with a Douglas B-66 destroyer, US F-105 Thunderchiefs unload their bombs over a military target in southern North Vietnam during Operation Rolling Thunder.

purely by its body count. Yet the lines between the VC and the civilian population were frequently blurred, hence search-and-destroy often had brutal consequences for civilian communities, creating alienation between the US troops and the very people they were supposed to be saving from communism. This in turn helped turn much US and international opinion against the war. During the Vietnam War, as historians frequently point out, US forces won every battle they fought, but the war for public confidence was a losing campaign, not least because the PAVN/VC were still managing to inflict significant casualties incrementally via ambushes, booby traps and snipers. In total, the USA would lose 58,163 troops in the conflict.

The Helicopter War

The Vietnam War was the not the first conflict to see the use of helicopters, but during this conflict rotary-wing aircraft were employed on a previously unimagined scale. Entire divisions were made 'airmobile', meaning that thousands of troops could be deployed simultaneously in massive air assault operations to remote locations. Helicopters such as the Bell UH-1 'Huey', Boeing CH-47 Chinook and Sikorsky CH-54 Tarhe offered logistical flexibility across a war zone characterized by complex jungle and mountainous terrain. They also enabled US forces to implement 'hammer-and-anvil' tactics, deploying one unit as an advancing force – the hammer – and another as a blocking force – the anvil – at a different location, squeezing the enemy between the two. In addition, Vietnam saw the application of helicopter gunships such as the AH-1G Cobra, these serving as 'aerial artillery' with their rockets, cannon and machine guns. More benignly, thousands of wounded allied troops would

> be saved by the efforts of 'medevac' (medical evacuation)
> helicopters, the pilots often flying into the midst of heavy
> firefights to rescue the wounded.

The search-and-destroy and insurgency phase of the war lasted until January 1968, when Giap – still in command of communist forces – launched a countrywide offensive, known as the Tet Offensive, hoping to spur a popular uprising in South Vietnam. Instead, the Tet Offensive was crushed emphatically over a period of several months. This time, the fighting was ferocious open warfare, including urban battles in cities such as Hue, tank vs tank warfare, and sieges around the Khe Sanh air base. Although the Tet Offensive resulted in massive casualties for the PAVN, and the virtual destruction of the VC, the intensity of the fighting after three years of US combat deployment convinced many that this was an unwinnable war. Thus from 1969, when Richard Nixon took the presidency, the USA began a progressive drawdown of forces, handing the struggle over to ARVN through the process of 'Vietnamization'.

The war between 1970 and 1975 saw the PAVN launch further major offensives, the largest (the Easter Offensive) in 1972, while the US-backed ARVN made incursions into neighbouring Cambodia and Laos against communist supply lines. In 1973, however, the USA withdrew its last combat troops, and South Vietnam stood mostly alone. The final act came in 1975, when the culminating PAVN offensive overran the ARVN lines and seized Saigon itself in late April, the last of US diplomatic, military and security personnel ignominiously ferried from rooftops to safety by US helicopters. Despite the efforts of the world's greatest superpower to prevent South Vietnam from falling to the communists, in 1975 North and South Vietnam became a unified, communist state.

THE MIDDLE EAST

The Middle East has had the unfortunate status of being in a state of near-constant conflict since 1945. The seeds of these wars are a seemingly intractable clash of religions, cultures and territorial interests, compounded by the retreat of colonialism, the significance of oil (the Middle East produces about 35 per cent of global oil output, but also holds about 70 per cent of global reserves) and powerful outside involvement.

Arab-Israeli Wars

Of all the motive forces behind the Middle Eastern wars, none is greater than the brittle and bloody relationship between Israel and its Arab neighbours. On 14 May 1948, the State of Israel was founded from part of the British mandate of Palestine as a homeland for the Jewish people. This act triggered an instant regional pushback from Arab states, who sought to extinguish the new-found state, and from the first day of its existence Israel was at war.

The First Arab–Israeli War ran from May 1948 to July 1949, and saw just 30,000 personnel of the fledgling Israel Defense Forces (IDF) pitted against the combined armed forces of Egypt, Iraq, Lebanon, Syria and Jordan, plus Palestinian Arabs. In an act of extraordinary military skill and motivation, which would come to characterize the Israeli way of war, the IDF triumphed, reversing initial Arab gains until by the time of a UN-mediated ceasefire in July 1949 Israel was in possession of all the former British mandate, including the West Bank and Gaza Strip.

Israel was safe, for now, but cross-border skirmishes and incidents were a regular occurrence between Israel and the surrounding Arab states. The next phase of open warfare came in 1956, triggered when the Egyptian President, Gamal Abdel Nasser, closed the Gulf of Aqaba, cutting off the movement of Israeli shipping from its

A US B-25 Stratofortress bomber unloads its formidable bomb load over North Vietnam during the Linebacker raids. Each aircraft could carry up to 32,000 kg (70,000 lb) of ordnance.

southern port of Eilat, and then nationalized the Suez Canal, at that time owned by Britain with major French investors. Fearing that Egypt was planning a renewed offensive against them and unnerved by the imposed restrictions on its maritime trade, Israel secretly plotted with Britain and France to resolve the issue in a coordinated fashion – the British were particularly keen to see the Canal returned to their ownership. Thus on 29 October 1956, the IDF invaded the Sinai Peninsula, pushing back the Egyptian forces, while Britain and France declared that they would intervene to seize and protect the Suez Canal, ostensibly to keep it open to international shipping during the time of war. On 31 October, a combined Anglo-French force began conducting major airborne deployments over Port Said and the Suez Canal, even as the confident IDF ploughed forwards and took over the Sinai.

What became known as the 'Suez Crisis' precipitated an outraged response from the international community. The US and Soviet superpowers, the British Parliament and much of the Islamic world were furious at the intervention, and Britain came under heavy financial and diplomatic pressure to stop the war. Bowing to the opposition, the Europeans were compelled to withdraw from Suez following a US/UN brokered ceasefire on 7 November; the Israelis also withdrew from their Sinai conquests in March 1957, having achieved their main purpose of freeing the Gulf of Aqaba for its shipping.

As would occur so often in the Arab–Israeli wars, one war would simply lay the groundwork for the next. Egypt in particular was looking for opportunities to reassert itself in the region. In May 1967, following Egypt's expulsion of US peacekeepers in the region, the Arab armies surrounding Israel appeared to be massing on the Israeli borders for offensive action. The Gulf of Aqaba was, once again, closed to Israeli shipping. The Israeli government decided that the best course of action this time was a pre-emptive strike against their enemies, and when it launched this, on 5 June 1967, they initiated an almost textbook demonstration of military superiority.

The action began with devastating early-morning Israeli airstrikes against the Arab air forces, destroying hundreds of aircraft in a matter of hours; Egypt almost didn't have an air force left by the end of the first day. Then IDF armour and infantry surged across the borders, and, despite heavy fighting in many places, overwhelmed the over-centralized Arab armies with their dynamic and often maverick tactical decision-making. Against Egypt, the IDF overran the entire Sinai Peninsula and established itself on the east bank of the Suez Canal. To the north, Israel took the strategically important Golan Heights from the Syrians, while the Jordanians were unable to stop Israel occupying East Jerusalem and the entire West Bank of the River Jordan. All this was achieved from 5–10 June, hence the conflict was labelled the Six-Day War.

With the Six-Day War, the IDF established itself as arguably the world's most professional and combat-proven modern army. It had also reshaped the map of the Middle East, with Israel literally doubling its territory and establishing more defendable borders. There was certainly now no peace. The 'War of Attrition', three-years of cross-border artillery bombardments and raids, kept Egypt and Israel on an active combat footing. Furthermore, from 1970, the new Egyptian president, Anwar Sadat, began planning a fresh Arab offensive against Israel, which was launched, with an impressive degree of surprise, on 6 October 1973, the Jewish Day of Atonement, or Yom Kippur.

The Egyptian attack was conducted with a new professionalism. Having driven across the Suez Canal in a sophisticated amphibious assault, the Egyptian army pushed into the Sinai and established defensive positions under a dense umbrella of Soviet-supplied SAM missiles, to hold back the Israeli Air Force (IAF), while the infantry were equipped with hundreds of portable AT-3 Sagger and RPG-7

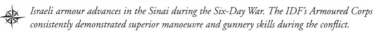 *Israeli armour advances in the Sinai during the Six-Day War. The IDF's Armoured Corps consistently demonstrated superior manoeuvre and gunnery skills during the conflict.*

anti-tank missiles to blunt the inevitable IDF armoured counter-attack. IDF losses were consequently heavy, and for a time it looked as if the Arabs might be on to a winning tactic. In the Golan Heights, Syria – the other key Arab player in the Yom Kippur War – also made some strong initial advances. But then both Egypt and Syria overreached themselves and the rebounding IDF vigorously exploited tactical openings. In the Golan Heights, an immense armoured engagement resulted in the Syrian army losing some 900 tanks and the IDF advancing to within a day's march of Damascus. In the Sinai, the Egyptian forces were outmanoeuvred, encircled and driven back, again with some large-scale armoured engagements – a 14 October battle involved some 2,000 tanks in action. The IDF units eventually pushed on over the Suez Canal, and only a US-negotiated ceasefire on 24 October brought the conflict, another huge Arab defeat, to a close on 24 October.

As with the Six-Day War, the Yom Kippur War did not bring peace. Terrorism and Israeli retaliations plagued the region constantly. In June 1982, Israel invaded southern Lebanon in an attempt to drive back the Palestine Liberation Organization (PLO) – the leading anti-Israel resistance movement in the Middle East – and Syrian forces that had intervened in Lebanon's bitter civil war, which had been raging since 1975. Establishing air superiority over Syrian air defences, the IDF pushed steadily on through southern Lebanon until it was investing Beirut. Although the operation was going the IDF's way militarily, international pressure built up on Israel to pull out, especially following the massacre, by Christian militias supported by the Israelis, of many hundreds of Palestinian refugees in the Sabra and Chatila refugee camps. In 1983, the Israelis withdrew and a multinational peacekeeping force was deployed to Beirut. In a dire example of how the Arab–Israeli wars could draw others in conflict, two huge bombings in Beirut subsequently killed 58 French soldiers and 241 US Marines.

The dump truck that destroyed the US Marine Corps barracks in Beirut in October 1983 was believed to have contained c.5,400 kg (12,000 lb) of explosives, the detonation completely collapsing the four-story building.

Iran–Iraq War

Although the Arab–Israeli Wars fuelled much of the conflict in the Middle East throughout the second half of the 20th century, those troubles were not the source of major wars in the region. Between 1980 and 1988, Iran and Iraq fought a war that killed as many as a million people and wounded hundreds of thousands more. The war began shortly after Saddam Hussein seized power in Iraq in July 1979. The invasion, launched in September 1980, was ostensibly about a dispute over the ownership of the Shatt al-Arab waterway, but was more likely related to Saddam Hussein's desire to increase his regional influence and domestic political power. Iran, meanwhile, had been militarily weakened by a recent revolution. The Iraqi Army, a relatively modern and professional force, initially made good headway in its campaign, but the Iranian response steadily intensified in its tenacity and brought the Iraqi onslaught to a halt. The war thereafter descended largely into a horrifying stalemate, both sides launching fruitless attacks that were high on human cost and low on territorial gain. The war even saw the use of chemical weapons, but eventually the UN sponsored a ceasefire in August 1988. Iraq's regional ambitions remained undimmed, however, and would lead to their invasion of Kuwait in 1990 (see next chapter).

GLOBAL WARS

While in this chapter we primarily focus on major international wars, in reality the world between 1945 and 1990 was a tapestry of conflicts, both major and minor, affecting every continent. Many of these conflicts were generated by post-1945 nationalist movements shrugging off the authority of European colonial powers, or fighting the civil wars left in the aftermath of independence.

The British, for example, fought a 12-year (1948–60) counter-insurgency campaign in Malaya to suppress the communist independence movement, the Malayan Races Liberation Army (MRLA). This effort was actually reasonably successful, in the process developing an effective body of British counter-insurgency doctrine and experience, but in 1957 Britain still granted Malaya its independence. The British also managed to suppress rebellion from the tribal 'Mau-Mau' movement in Kenya between 1953 and 1955, partly through the intelligent if brutal cooperation of local peoples. (Kenya became an independent Commonwealth country in 1963.)

The longest of Britain's continuous deployments (in history, not just the 20th century), however, was far closer to home. Operation *Banner* – the British military and security operation in Northern Ireland – began in 1969 and was sustained until 2007. What began as a welcomed mission to separate warring Catholic and Protestant communities became, in the eyes of Catholic nationalists represented militarily by the Irish Republican Army (IRA), a hated occupation. The result was an incessant weekly grind of bombings, shootings, assassinations and ambushes, mainly in Northern Ireland although they also spread to the British mainland. By the time the 'Troubles' ended, brought about mainly by the signing of the Good Friday Agreement in 1998, some 722 British military personnel had died in paramilitary attacks, with 719 deaths from other causes and more than 6,000 wounded.

In the early 1980s, Britain fought a very different war from the counter-insurgency and counter-terrorism operations that characterized the campaigns above. In March 1982, Argentina invaded South Georgia and the Falkland Islands, British possessions in the deep South Atlantic, fulfilling what Argentina saw as a long-standing claim over the islands. The initial occupation, despite a brief spell of ferocious resistance from a small group of Royal Marines, was achieved quickly and victory was proclaimed. In a matter of days, however, Britain put together a powerful Task Force of naval, air and land power, and sailed the 13,000 km (8,100 miles) to reclaim the islands. It would be a close-fought campaign. Argentine air power took a heavy toll on British shipping, sinking seven vessels, including the *Atlantic Conveyor* merchant ship that carried almost all the infantry's Chinook heavy-lift transport helicopters. Yet the British managed to put ashore and, after a long 'yomp' across the Falklands and several infantry battles, Port Stanley, the Falklands' capital, was liberated on 14 June. The victory stood as the high point of British military fortunes following World War II.

Compounding the loss of Indochina, the French also fought a long and ultimately losing war between 1954 and 1967 to retain its colony of Algeria, against the Front Libération de Nationale (FLN). To the south, sub-Saharan Africa meanwhile suffered under some of the bloodiest civil and post-colonial conflicts of the century, especially in the Congo, Biafra, Angola, Mozambique, Guinea and Rhodesia. The Indian subcontinent, plagued by violence since independence and partition in 1947, also experienced repeated turmoil. India fought China in a border war in 1962 and Pakistan in 1947–58, 1965 and again in 1971. The 1971 war saw Indian and Pakistani armoured forces lock horns in one of the biggest tank battles since World War II, fought in southern Kashmir on 6 December 1971. India eventually claimed victory, a triumph that led to the independence of Bangladesh.

Half a world away, Central and South America were plagued by numerous revolutionary wars, Latin America providing fertile ground for extremist insurgencies and dictatorial governments on both the left and the right of politics. The Cuban revolution of 1959 under Fidel Castro embedded Soviet-style communism in Latin America, and began an ideological struggle that affected almost every nation, in some cases the civil conflicts running for decades, not years. Some of the worst-affected states included Nicaragua, Guatemala, Venezuela, Colombia, Bolivia, Uruguay, Chile and Argentina. Most of the fighting consisted of classic insurgency small-unit actions, but they often placed the civilian populations in a precarious and terrifying position between warring sides.

And what of the Soviet Union, the superpower whose shadow is perceived in the background of many of the conflicts described in this chapter? In 1989–91, precipitated by a groundswell of economic, political and social factors, communism unravelled in the Soviet Union and Eastern Europe, leading most symbolically to the fall of the Berlin Wall in November 1989, German reunification in 1990, and the dissolution of the Soviet Union in 1991. One of the factors that fed into the collapse of the Soviet Union was the disastrous war it fought in Afghanistan between 1979 and 1989.

 The destroyer HMS Sheffield *burns uncontrollably after being hit an Exocet anti-ship missile off the Falkland Islands on 4 May 1982.*

 *Contra guerrillas in Nicaragua, 1987. The Contras fought the Nicaraguan government for more than a decade, and received financial and material backing from the United States.*

Soviet forces invaded Afghanistan in strength on 25 December 1979, attempting to maintain a pro-Soviet regime in Kabul against Islamic mujahideen ('holy warriors'). While the Soviets brought with them their full conventional military panoply, including gunships, artillery and heavy armour, they ended up locked in a guerrilla war in remote and often mountainous terrain, a type of warfare for which they were ill-suited. Although the Soviets certainly imposed heavy casualties upon both the mujahideen and the unfortunate civilian population, they were never able to gain proper traction over the enemy. Thus, ten years later, with c.14,500 Soviet soldiers dead and nearly 54,000 wounded, the Soviets finally gave up the struggle and withdrew, leaving Afghanistan to experience further pain in a civil war – one that led to the victory of the extremist Taliban in 1996.

The Soviet debacle in Afghanistan, the US strategic defeat in Vietnam, the expulsion of many former colonial powers – the period from 1945–1990 signalled a transformation in world order. Although there were certainly many conventional wars during this period, steadily the battleground appeared to be shifting towards insurgency and counter-insurgency, low-level wars with outcomes decided more by duration than by strength of arms. As we then move through the 1990s and into the 2000s, however, modern warfare became even more complex to fight.

CHAPTER 7
THE NEW AGE OF WARFARE

From the 1991 Gulf War to the present day, warfare has been a complex tapestry of civil wars, outrageous acts of terrorism and major international conflicts. Looking ahead, advanced digital technology seems to be the shaping force behind the future of conflict, but older forms of war-fighting remain persistent, and will likely remain so well into the future.

On 2 August 1990, the armed forces of Iraqi dictator Saddam Hussein rolled over their south-eastern border into neighbouring Kuwait. Although the Iraqi Army had been massing on the border for several days, the world interpreted this build-up as little more than sabre-rattling; Saddam was attempting to make his diminutive neighbour capitulate to a series of demands relating to disputes over oilfields and Iraqi debts from the Iran–Iraq War. The international community, however, had thoroughly misinterpreted Saddam's intentions. Within 48 hours, Kuwait had been fully occupied and annexed by Iraq.

Yet if there had been intelligence failures on the part of the world powers, Saddam's belief that Kuwait would remain the 19th province of Iraq was equally misguided. Spurred by the concern that Iraq might potentially invade Saudi Arabia, and thereby destabilize the foundations of global oil supply, in August–November 1990 a large international Coalition was formed, led by the USA as the dominant player, and deployed en masse to Saudi Arabia as part

A US B-2 Spirit bomber, one of the new generation of 'stealth aircraft' with exceptionally low radar detection profiles, drops a string of Mk 82 bombs during a training exercise in 1994.

of the defensively oriented Operation *Desert Shield.* Despite UN sanctions, an economic blockade and the military thunderclouds gathering on his horizon, Saddam nevertheless held defiantly on to his new acquisition. On 18 November, the United Nations passed Resolution 678, which gave Iraqi forces a deadline of 15 January 1991 to withdraw from Kuwait or be expelled by military force.

FULL SPECTRUM DOMINANCE

On 16 January 1991, with Iraqi forces still unmoved in Kuwait, the Coalition moved to a war footing. Coalition ground forces now numbered more than 280,000 combat troops and 2,200 tanks from more than 16 nations, plus hundreds of fighters, bombers and strike aircraft, flying from land bases across Europe and the Middle East and from US carriers in the Persian Gulf. From 16 January until 22 February, the Coalition unleashed one of the greatest air campaigns since World War II, with relentless round-the-clock sorties as well as naval Tomahawk cruise missiles striking Iraqi military installations, command-and-control systems, air bases, storage depots, armoured vehicles, command bunkers and other targets with lethal precision. This 42-day air campaign, which involved 100,000 Coalition sorties, devastated Iraq's military functionality. The Iraqi Air Force was effectively wiped out (140 aircraft and pilots actually took off and fled to Iran) and retaliation via Scud ballistic missiles was concerning but ultimately inconsequential.

Then, on 24 February, the ground offensive component of Operation *Desert Storm* was unleashed – a huge three-pronged advance by corps-strength coalition formations through Iraq and into Kuwait. Prior to the invasion, there had been much Coalition and media concern about what Saddam Hussein predicted would be 'the mother of all battles'. Iraq, after all, had one of the most substantial armies in the Middle East – *c*.900,000 troops, many of them combat experienced from the Iran–Iraq War, 5,700 tanks and 3,700 artillery pieces. Yet as quickly became apparent, Iraqi forces were completely outclassed by the professionalism, dynamic command-and-control, weapon systems and tactics of the Coalition. Entire Iraqi battalions of troops were battered into surrender by terrifying air strikes. Armoured vehicles would often be destroyed by air-dropped precision guided munitions (PGMs) within minutes of moving from cover, their positions detected by superior Coalition reconnaissance and surveillance systems (including satellite surveillance). Iraqi tanks that faced the US M1 Abrams or British Challengers were often destroyed by superior gunnery before they had even made visual acquisition of their enemy. Iraqi infantry who chose to fight, including the supposedly elite Iraqi Republican Guard, were quickly smashed, scattered or compelled to surrender by Coalition artillery and manoeuvre. To all intents and purposes, it was a rout. The Coalition secured victory within just 100 hours of the ground campaign beginning. A ceasefire was signed, and those Iraqi forces still standing were compelled to leave Kuwait.

For the USA, this relatively 'clean' victory in many ways seemed to exorcise the ghosts of the Vietnam War. It appeared to demonstrate the holy grail of what some military thinkers referred to as 'Full Spectrum Dominance', indicating a military's overwhelming superiority within all arenas of the battlespace – land, air, sea, space – through a combination of advanced and integrated technologies (especially networked communications and surveillance), professionalism of forces and undefeatable firepower. For some, Operation *Desert Storm* augured a new era in the history of warfare, one in which the modern US armed services and their Coalition partners would be unassailable. As history would show, however, such expectations were premature.

POST-COMMUNIST WARS

With the collapse of communism, and the break-up of the Soviet Union, the entire world order was transformed, not least militarily. What had been the Soviet Army was steadily divided up between new independent states and states forming part of the Russian Federation, and years of turmoil and weakness followed. The Armed Forces of the Russian Federation could still regard itself as one of the largest militaries in the world – by 1996 it had 670,000 troops directly under Moscow's control, and thousands of armoured vehicles, artillery pieces, missiles and aircraft, plus its nuclear inventory. But the reality on the ground was less auspicious. Economic hardship, corruption and a pervasive culture of bullying weakened both the morale and the combat capability of Russian troops. Desertion became endemic; there were numerous cases of young conscripts being literally bullied to death; much advanced equipment sat rusting and unmaintained, or was stolen.

 US M1 Abrams tanks push forward at speed during Operation Desert Storm, 1991. The Abrams is a third-generation tank, with a multi-fuel turbine engine and advanced computerized fire control.

Bullying in the Russian Army

The bullying of new conscripts has, historically, often been part of military cultures, especially those with poor standards of professionalism and low morale. In the Soviet and post-communist Russian Army, it reached truly grotesque levels, possibly resulting in the deaths of hundreds of young conscripts every year through either suicide or direct violence. The phenomenon was known as *dedovshchina*, or 'grandfatherism', referring to the fact that soldiers who were at least halfway through their military service were called *dedy* (grandfathers), with complete authority over the lives of the new recruits or *molodoy* (youngsters). Essentially, the *molody* became the brutalized servants of the *dedy*, subject to daily ritual humiliation, confiscations of money and food, and severe, sometimes lethal, beatings or 'accidents' if the young recruit failed to please his master. *Dedovshchina* had a significant effect on Russian Army morale, recruitment and retention in the 1990s, and joining the armed forces became something to be avoided. Since this time, the Russian Army has made concerted efforts to stamp out the worst excesses.

The fallen nature of the former Soviet army was nowhere more terribly demonstrated than in Russia's war in Chechnya in 1994–6. From 1991, secessionist movements gathered pace in the republic of Chechnya, a mountainous country in the North Caucasus, leading to an anti-Russian coup and declared independence from the Russian Federation. In December 1994, Russian forces invaded Chechnya in strength, confident that their preponderance of troops, armour, artillery and air power would soon bring the recalcitrant republic back into the fold. Instead, they found themselves facing resistance of stone-faced tenacity, the Chechens utilizing a mix of conventional and insurgency warfare to inflict severe casualties upon the Russian units. The war became one of atrocity and counter-atrocity. For example, the Russians levelled the city of Grozny in their grinding campaign to secure it, during which campaign they lost nearly 2,000 tanks to street-level anti-tank ambushes.

Although the Russians eventually took Grozny, they nevertheless found themselves locked into a prolonged guerrilla war from which they struggled to escape. Eventually, in May 1997, a provisional peace treaty was signed and the Russians withdrew, leaving behind a possible 80,000 dead Chechens and 5,700 of their own troops.

This would not be the last Russian incursion into Chechnya. Russia would fight another, far longer conflict in Chechnya between 1999 – the year in which Vladimir Putin became the Russian prime minister – and 2009, triggered when Chechen-based Islamic *jihadists* invaded the Russian republic of Dagestan in August 1999. The conventional phase of the war lasted from August 1999 until May 2000 and, as previously, was ferocious. Yet the Russian army was by the early 2000s a changing animal. A programme of military reforms was starting to bear fruit in improved tactics, and the Russian reliance upon firepower rather than close-quarters tactics meant reduced casualties. Grozny fell after just over a month of siege, and thereafter the war spread into the mountainous regions, but by the spring of 2000 most of the major centres of resistance had been suppressed. Russia would go on to fight a lengthy guerrilla war of shifting intensity, and experienced the fallout of Chechen terrorism on its own soil, but in April 2009 the counter-insurgency phase of operations was declared complete.

The war in Chechnya was not the only conflict seeded by the break-up of communism. During the 1980s, Yugoslavia experienced a rise in ethnic, religious and regional tension as communism's iron bonds began to soften. The problems intensified with the election of the violently nationalistic Slobodan Milošević as leader of Serbia in 1987. Milošević's vision for a 'Greater Serbia' led, in the early 1990s, to an unsuccessful attempt to carve up Yugoslavia into various federated and regional identities, and by the spring of 1992 the now former Yugoslavia was plunged into a civil war that tore its peoples apart for more than four years. The war was particularly hard on the civilian populations (as wars always are); many towns and villages were destroyed in the processes of ethnic cleansing, particularly in Bosnia and Herzegovina, whose capital, Sarajevo, enduring a siege by Bosnian Serb forces that lasted just under three years and four weeks. The international community endeavoured to stay out of the war until the massacre, again by Bosnian Serbs, of 7,000 Bosniak men from Srebrenica in July 1995, after which NATO responded at first by imposing a no-fly zone against Serbian aircraft and later by actual air strikes on Bosnian Serb targets. This intervention eventually pushed the warring parties to the negotiation table, and the Dayton Accords, signed in December 1995, brought the conflict to an uneasy end, albeit with the deployment of 60,000 peacekeepers.

The former Yugoslavia remained a restless entity throughout the 1990s, and in the last years of the decade the ethnic tensions once again flashed into war, this time centred around the Serbian province of Kosovo. Between 1996 and 1998, the ethnic Albanian Kosovo Liberation Army (KLA) began a steadily escalating campaign of guerrilla resistance against what they saw as encroachments of Serbian authority. This led, in 1998, to a full-blown Serbian and Yugoslav campaign in Kosovo, one that soon descended into horrifying acts of ethnic cleansing and the eventual expulsion of almost all ethnic Albanians from the territory. Only after an 11-week NATO bombing campaign against Serbian targets was a peace accord finally agreed and hundreds of thousands of Kosovan

Albanians allowed to return. The former Yugoslavia remains in a state of tension to this day.

AFGHANISTAN AND IRAQ

If the Gulf War of 1990–1 was the supreme demonstration of Western military superiority, the wars in Afghanistan and Iraq from 2001 until, in one form or another, the present day, have been a sobering corrective to any enduring celebration. They also represent one of the major conflict generators of the modern world – that between the West (or similarly oriented cultures) and radical Islam.

Islamic terrorism was a persistent phenomenon globally from the 1970s until the early 2000s. But little prepared the world for what occurred on 11 September 2001, when Al-Qaeda terrorists hijacked four US domestic airliners in flight, crashing two into the World Trade Center – both the towers subsequently collapsed – one into the Pentagon, while the fourth came down in Pennsylvania. A total of 2,977 people were killed on US soil that day, by far the worst terrorist atrocity in history.

Al-Qaeda

Al-Qaeda (literally 'The Base') is an extremist militant Islamic organization that was formed in the late 1980s by Osama bin Laden, who would go on to mastermind the 9/11 attacks on the USA. The group emerged in Afghanistan during the late stages of the war against the Soviets, and after the conflict took its focus as *jihad* (holy war) against the USA, Western culture, and against Islamic states and peoples who courted Western lifestyles and governments. During the first half of the 1990s it was based in Sudan, but relocated its headquarters to Afghanistan in 1996, where it grew in strength, reach and

the boldness of its activities. With a membership numbering in
the tens of thousands, scattered globally, Al-Qaeda committed
a series of increasingly audacious attacks, including the
bombing of the US embassies in Nairobi, Kenya, and Dar es
Salaam, Tanzania in 1998 and a suicide bomb attack against
the US destroyer *Cole* in Aden, Yemen, in 2000. Yet it was the
9/11 attacks in the USA that made Al-Qaeda the most hunted
terrorist organization on the planet. Even in the face of a vast
international military and intelligence campaign, and the
discovery and killing of Osama bin Laden in 2011 in Pakistan
by a US Special Forces team, Al-Qaeda has proved a sinewy
organization, with a diffuse and decentralized structure that is
difficult to eradicate.

The attacks galvanized the USA in a way not seen since
Pearl Harbor. They were soon joined by key allies among the
international community, who together looked to respond in force,
not just against Al-Qaeda but also against those who harboured
and protected them. The first target was Afghanistan, where Al-
Qaeda based itself under the sympathetic umbrella of the Taliban
government. After the Taliban refused to hand over bin Laden,
US direct involvement escalated, first focusing on providing CIA
and Special Forces support for the anti-Taliban Northern Alliance
group within Afghanistan, but quickly progressing to air strikes and
large-scale troop deployments.

Together, the US forces and the Northern Alliance quickly
overthrew the Taliban as part of the Operation *Enduring Freedom*,
seizing both Kabul and Kandahar in the process. In December
2001, US, Afghan and Pakistani troops fought a major battle in
Tora Bora, bin Laden's mountainous cave complex stronghold

just to the south-west of Jalalabad. Despite inflicting heavy casualties on Al-Qaeda, and dropping tons of rock-crumbling ordnance on to the mountain, the mission was unsuccessful and bin Laden escaped.

The operations in 2001 were just the beginning of what would become the USA's longest operational deployment in its history – some 14 years. After the initial overthrow of the Taliban government, the campaign broke down into two main phases. First, the US forces focused on fighting the Taliban in their rural and mountainous strongholds while also attempting to rebuild Afghanistan's infrastructure, military and government along lines that would resist Taliban return. This phase, which lasted from roughly 2001 to 2009, also saw the USA joined in the war by a host of international allies, together labelled the International Security Assistance Force (ISAF). In the subsequent phase, inspired by frustrations to control the deteriorating security situation, President Barack Obama (in his election year) authorized a major surge in US troops numbers – an additional 30,000 troops were deployed – focusing on winning the counter-insurgency war. This phase progressed, with uncertain results, until 2012, when the last of the 'surge' troops were withdrawn. Two years later, US and NATO forces formally announced the end of combat operations.

What had this, the longest of US wars, achieved? There were positives: Afghanistan had held free elections and much of the population was no longer under the dire extremist rule of the Taliban. And yet, in many ways the war appeared to be a strategic defeat. Very extensive areas of the country remained unpacified, with the Taliban simply filling the vacuum left by the departing Americans; civilian casualties from Taliban attacks are high; the government is largely corrupt and unstable; there is little infrastructural improvement, despite the USA spending $38 billion alone in-country between 2001 and 2009; and the country produces 90 per cent of the world's opium. It is hard to find a metric for success.

Before asking why this occurred, we should also reflect upon the other major conflict in the USA's 'War on Terror': the invasion of Iraq in 2003. In the aftermath of 9/11, the US President, George W. Bush, turned his focus to Iraq, which was still under the iron rule of Saddam Hussein. Iraq was accused of possessing nuclear, biological and chemical Weapons of Mass Destruction (WMDs) – a charge that later was proved false – and of sponsoring international terrorism. Saddam was compelled to admit UN weapons inspectors. Following what was perceived as acts of non-compliance with the inspection, Saddam was given, on 17 March 2003, a 48-hour ultimatum to step down and leave Iraq, or face forcible military expulsion – large-scale US and allied forces were already in the region in preparation. On 20 March, more than 177,000 coalition troops crossed the border into Iraq; unlike the previous invasion into Iraq, this one was set on regime change.

Unlike the 1991 operation, this time the coalition forces went straight for the jugular with little pre-emptive air campaign, although air power swarmed constantly over and ahead of the advance. US forces pushed on quickly to Baghdad, taking control of the capital by 9 April – Saddam had fled by this time – the same day on which British forces seized Al-Basrah, Iraq's main port. Saddam's home town Tikrit was captured on 13 April. (The dictator himself was finally captured in December 2003, subsequently convicted by Iraqi authorities of crimes against humanity, and hanged on 30 December 2006.) Feeling empowered with victory, on 1 May President Bush announced the end of major combat operations aboard the aircraft carrier USS *Abraham Lincoln*, which displayed a banner reading 'Mission Accomplished'. Revealingly, on the same day the US Secretary of Defense Donald Rumsfeld also proclaimed that the military campaign in Afghanistan was essentially over.

 A Cougar MRAP (Mine Resistant Ambush Protected) vehicle, wrecked by an improvised explosive device (IED) in Al-Anbar, Iraq, although as intended by design the crew compartment has stayed largely intact.

Both declarations were profoundly misguided. In Iraq, the security situation quickly unravelled in subsequent chaos. New factions, militias, warlords and insurgents emerged, and began prosecuting an extreme guerrilla war both against the Iraqi people and against the US and allied forces. Dozens of improvised explosive devices (IEDs) would explode every day around the country. Ambushes and assassinations were constant. The only priority for much of the population was to survive another day. The US forces were also suffering heavily: by the time President Bush declared 'Mission Accomplished', there had been about 150 coalition deaths. By 2007, it was more than 3,000. The Iraq War became a millstone around the USA's neck.

It took until December 2011 for US and international combat forces to withdraw from Iraq. By this point, 4,496 US soldiers, 179 British soldiers and 139 soldiers from other nations had been killed; the cost to Iraqi security forces was 17,690 killed. Total Coalition/Iraqi military wounded was *c*.117,000 – frontline casevac (casualty evacuation) and medical treatment was delivered with such excellence that 90 per cent of Coalition casualties in both Iraq and Afghanistan would survive their injuries.

Yet 2011 did not see the end of international, and particularly US, involvement in Iraq. The situation in the country was still nowhere near what we might term stable, and this year saw the ascendant phase of a new extremist Islamic insurgency group in Iraq. Formed in 2006, Islamic State in Iraq (ISI) was an evolution of the former Al-Qaeda in Iraq group. ISI was a transnational organization dedicated to the establishment of fundamentalist Islamic rule in the Middle East. It flourished in the turbulence of post-invasion Iraq and in neighbouring Syria, which was at this point gripped by civil war (see below). Led from 2010 by Abu Bakr al-Baghdadi, ISI established a base in Syria at Al-Raqqah, and in 2013 relabelled itself Islamic State in Iraq and the Levant (ISIL). Its name alone gave a clear indication of its ambitions.

ISIL went on to shock the world in two ways. The first was the extreme cruelty of its methods, with mass executions and hideous torture openly displayed as part of its modus operandi; fear was a critical tool for both recruitment and subjugation. The second was its unforeseen success. By May 2015, ISIL had established direct control over a great swathe of Iraq and Syria, a total of 106,000 sq. km (41,000 sq. miles) of territory and 8–12 million people. In battle, ISIL captured major Iraqi cities, including Al-Fallujah, Al-Ramadi and Mosul, showing itself as militarily confident. But 2015 was the high water mark of ISIL success. In 2014, a US-led coalition was formed – the Combined Joint Task Force – and Operation *Inherent Resolve* (CJTF–OIR) began hitting ISIL with air strikes, while Special Forces and artillery supported anti-ISIL ground operations by local forces in both Iraq and Syria. Gradually, the effort of fighting on multiple fronts became unsustainable for ISIL. It steadily lost almost all of its territorial gains in Iraq, although it only gave up the bigger towns and cities after horrendous and lengthy close-quarters urban warfare. Al-Baghdadi himself committed suicide by detonating an explosive suicide vest on 26 October 2019, having been trapped by US Special Forces at Barish, Idlib Province, Syria.

The war against ISIL certainly crushed what was once a widespread and feared organization. But insurgency groups tend to be many-headed beasts, and the remnants and sub-groups of ISIL are scattered widely across the Middle East, North Africa, Afghanistan, Pakistan and elsewhere. Still active through acts of terrorism and involvement in other people's wars, ISIL is likely to be a persistent global security threat for the future.

THE ARAB SPRING AND SYRIA

The second decade of the 2000s was a period of extraordinary social and political convulsions in the Middle East and North Africa. Many of the Arab states were authoritarian and non-democratic by nature, but in 2010 and 2011 a ripple of pro-democracy uprisings ran through the region, specifically in Tunisia, Egypt, Bahrain, Yemen and Syria. These are collectively known as the events of the 'Arab Spring'. In all instances, the uprisings produced violence of varying degrees between the people and the state security apparatus, and also between civilian and paramilitary groups divided upon religious, political or ethnic grounds. Outcomes were far from uniform. Egypt and Tunisia, for example, came out of the Arab Spring with new directly elected governments. Bahrain's revolt was quashed in little over a month by the state. In the cases of Libya and Syria, however, the political revolts expanded to become outright wars that, much like the fight against ISIL, quickly drew international players into the conflicts.

An armed insurrection against Libya's dictator Muammar al-Qaddafi began in early 2011. The rebel forces, composed of a jigsaw puzzle of civilians, paramilitary groups and professional military defectors, were quickly outmatched by Gaddafi's conventional army, and driven back to the east. But then a UN resolution on 17 March not only established a no-fly zone over Libya (directly shutting down Libyan Air Force operations against the rebels), but also authorized 'all necessary measures' to protect civilians. The outcome was that NATO unleashed its air power on Libyan ground forces, an action that in turn allowed the rebels to resume offensive action in August. This time, they pushed through and took the Libyan capital Tripoli, Gaddafi fleeing from the city and from power; he was eventually captured and killed by rebel troops in Surt in October 2011.

Unfortunately for the people of Libya, Gaddafi's ousting and execution did not bring their early hopes for stability and peace to fruition. Instead, the country progressively broke into various power factions and rival governments. This situation fuelled another civil war that is ongoing at the time of writing, the fighting a tapestry of interests, warlords and outside involvement.

A month after the first revolts in Libya, Syria also witnessed stirring pro-democracy unrest, here directed against the autocratic government of Bashar al-Assad. The escalation of this unrest to a consuming civil war took place in a matter of months. What has been shocking has been the intensity of the fighting and the scale of the destruction, with an estimated half a million deaths to date, mainly among the beleaguered civilian population. The battlefields have come to rival those of World War II – the city of Aleppo, for example, has been referred to as 'Syria's Stalingrad', much of the city reduced to absolute ruins by more than four years of fighting and bombardment. The conflict has also come to have a thoroughly international flavour. Al-Assad's regime receives the support of both Iran and, strikingly, Russia, which began delivering military aid from 2011 but from 2015 provided direct military action, principally in the form of air strikes. Russia's presence raised the stakes of Western involvement through the CJTF-OIR, which launched air strikes mainly on ISIL targets but also on government forces. The anti-Assad alliance includes Qatar, Turkey, Saudi Arabia, the USA, Britain, the EU and the Arab League, although the various and often conflicting agendas of the rebel groups makes international interventions a Gordian knot of ethical decision-making. The Syrian civil war remains ongoing in 2020, although by this stage the al-Assad government appears securely in power, with the rebel forces confined in relatively small areas of land in the far north and far south of the country.

FUTURE WAR

Conflicts such as those in Afghanistan, Iraq and Syria are sobering counterpoints to the relatively 'clean' action (at least operationally) of Operation *Desert Storm* back in 1991. Indeed, if the latter conflict exorcized the ghosts of Vietnam, Afghanistan and Iraq have conjured them fully back into life, reminding us that modern insurgencies, tangled by an irreducible spectrum of combatants and interests, remain largely beyond the control of even a superpower like the USA.

There are, however, signs that the wars of the future will likely be very different from those of the immediate past. For a start, at the time of writing the international strategic balance of power contains hints of potential future change. Superpower China, free from involvement in costly wars in the Middle East and Afghanistan, is surging forwards with its military investment, its army increasing in size and its technologies growing in sophistication. Several of these technologies are igniting concern in the West, not least the hypersonic Dong-Feng 21D anti-ship ballistic missile – nicknamed by some the 'carrier killer' – and a satellite-destroying system, the SC-19. Together, these weapons threaten two of the USA's key military assets, namely aircraft carriers and satellite navigation/surveillance. Russia also has some potent new technologies in its arsenal, especially the Avangard hypersonic ballistic missile system, which by flying at 20 times the speed of sound is almost impossible to intercept. Russia, like China, has also developed a hypersonic anti-ship missile, the 3M22 Zircon.

But the West is now also putting its foot to the floor in terms of military innovation. Indeed, the battlespace of the future is one likely to be transformed by a profound range of technological innovations at both tactical and strategic levels. We can make some informed predictions from current developments. Coordinated swarms of weaponized drones will burst through the windows of buildings and then hunt the enemy inside with extraordinary speed. Soldiers will literally be able to see around corners with light-bending goggles. Unmanned Aerial Vehicles (UAVs – see feature box) will not only constitute the bulk of combat aviation, even on aircraft carriers, but will also have autonomous or near-autonomous powers of engagement through onboard artificial intelligence (AI) systems. AI will find its way into a host of other weapon systems, such as remotely deployed anti-armour missile systems, land mines and even armoured vehicles. Even the most extreme vision of military technology – that of armies of robot soldiers – no longer appears implausibly futuristic.

UAVs

Unmanned Aerial Vehicles (UAVs) – remote-controlled aircraft without a human pilot on board – are actually not a modern invention. Initial experiments in UAV technology can be seen during the first two decades of the 20th century, largely in the context of building pilotless drones for anti-aircraft gunnery training. It was during the Cold War, however, that UAVs became more of a battlefield presence, mainly as a way of performing detailed surveillance over enemy battlespace without putting a human pilot at risk. UAVs were used in this capacity by the USA in the Vietnam War and by the Israelis during the Arab–Israeli Wars of the 1960s and 70s, the Israelis also applying UAVs to decoy enemy SAM batteries away from piloted combat aircraft. During the 1990s and early 2000s, Unmanned Combat Aerial Vehicles (UCAVs) – UAVs capable of mounting and launching ordnance – began to make their appearance in significant numbers, particularly operated in hunter-killer roles by US forces. These weapons became core technologies in the 'War on Terror', loitering at altitude for hours on end over the combat zone or restricted areas, and taking out point or high-

 An MQ-1 Predator, armed with AGM-114 Hellfire missiles, flies a combat mission over southern Afghanistan. Drones such as this can be flown by operators thousands of miles from the battlefield via datalink.

value targets when identified using the UCAV's own onboard surveillance and monitoring equipment. Such are the advances in global communications that pilots based in hubs in the USA literally fly UCAV combat missions over Afghanistan in real time. The future generations of UAVs/UCAVs promise an ever-greater diversity of types, ranging from tiny insect-sized craft used for covert surveillance inside buildings through to strategic bombers. Given their capabilities, a question mark hangs over the future of piloted combat aviation.

There will also likely be innovations in tactics. The Russians, for example, are viewed by some as being proponents of future 'hybrid warfare', achieving military objectives through a mix of conventional war-fighting (often conducted by sponsored para-militaries rather than one's own forces), insurgency, propaganda, political manoeuvring and, crucially, cyberwarfare. While it is a matter of debate whether hybrid warfare is really anything new – military campaigns have always consisted of more than the sum of the fighting – what is undeniable is that cyberwarfare will certainly be a battleground of the future. We are already seeing this in action. In 2017, numerous public and private organizations across the Ukraine – including banks, government websites, and utility companies – were hit by a concentrated cyberattack, likely with the involvement of Russian intelligence agencies. In 2010, the technology within the Iranian nuclear programme was serious damaged by the 'Stuxnet' computer malware, which is credited to a joint development of the USA and Israel.

The battles in cyberspace, compared to the brutal clashes of steel and fire we have journeyed through in this history, might seem somewhat more benign, even bloodless, versions of warfare. Yet such is our world's utter dependence upon digital systems and data processing that what might begin as a cyberwar could in fact lead to traditional conflict, once again on a global scale.

INDEX